ROUTLEDGE LIBRARY EDITIONS:
LITERACY

Volume 23



# FROM PICTURES TO LETTERS

# FROM PICTURES TO LETTERS

## First Steps in the Teaching of Reading and Writing

ELLEN WALPOLE

Routledge
Taylor & Francis Group
LONDON AND NEW YORK

First published in 1937 by Kegan Paul

This edition first published in 2018
by Routledge
2 Park Square, Milton Park, Abingdon, Oxon OX14 4RN

and by Routledge
711 Third Avenue, New York, NY 10017

*Routledge is an imprint of the Taylor & Francis Group, an informa business*



*British Library Cataloguing in Publication Data*
A catalogue record for this book is available from the British Library

ISBN: 978-1-138-55984-4 (Set)
ISBN: 978-0-203-70159-1 (Set) (ebk)
ISBN: 978-0-8153-7263-9 (Volume 23) (hbk)
ISBN: 978-0-8153-7366-7 (Volume 23) (pbk)
ISBN: 978-1-351-23606-5 (Volume 23) (ebk)

**Publisher's Note**
The publisher has gone to great lengths to ensure the quality of this reprint but points out that some imperfections in the original copies may be apparent.

**Disclaimer**
The publisher has made every effort to trace copyright holders and would welcome correspondence from those they have been unable to trace.

*PSYCHE MINIATURES*
*General Series No. 85*

# FROM PICTURES TO LETTERS

# FROM PICTURES TO LETTERS

## First Steps in the Teaching of Reading and Writing

BY

ELLEN WALPOLE

LONDON
KEGAN PAUL, TRENCH, TRUBNER & Co., Ltd.,
BROADWAY HOUSE, CARTER LANE, E.C.
1937

# BASIC ENGLISH

## PERATIONS 100 ETC.

COME GET GIVE GO KEEP LET MAKE PUT SEEM TAKE BE DO HAVE SAY SEE SEND MAY WILL ABOUT ACROSS AFTER AGAINST AMONG AT BEFORE BETWEEN BY DOWN FROM IN OFF ON OVER THROUGH TO UNDER UP WITH AS FOR OF TILL THAN A THE ALL ANY EVERY NO OTHER SOME SUCH THAT THIS I HE YOU WHO AND BECAUSE BUT OR IF THOUGH WHILE HOW WHEN WHERE WHY AGAIN EVER FAR FORWARD HERE NEAR NOW OUT STILL THEN THERE TOGETHER WELL ALMOST ENOUGH EVEN LITTLE MUCH NOT ONLY QUITE SO VERY TOMORROW YESTERDAY NORTH SOUTH EAST WEST PLEASE YES

## THINGS

### 400 General

ACCOUNT ACT ADDITION ADJUSTMENT ADVERTISEMENT AGREEMENT AIR AMOUNT AMUSEMENT ANIMAL ANSWER APPARATUS APPROVAL ARGUMENT ART ATTACK ATTEMPT ATTENTION ATTRACTION AUTHORITY BACK BALANCE BASE BEHAVIOUR BELIEF BIRTH BIT BITE BLOOD BLOW BODY BRASS BREAD BREATH BROTHER BUILDING BURN BURST BUSINESS BUTTER CANVAS CARE CAUSE CHALK CHANCE CHANGE CLOTH COAL COLOUR COMFORT COMMITTEE COMPANY COMPARISON COMPETITION CONDITION CONNECTION CONTROL COOK COPPER COPY CORK COTTON COUGH COUNTRY COVER CRACK CREDIT CRIME CRUSH CRY CURRENT CURVE DAMAGE DANGER DAUGHTER DAY DEATH DEBT DECISION DEGREE DESIGN DESIRE DESTRUCTION DETAIL DEVELOPMENT DIGESTION DIRECTION DISCOVERY DISCUSSION DISEASE DISGUST DISTANCE DISTRIBUTION DIVISION DOUBT DRINK DRIVING DUST EARTH EDGE

EDUCATION EFFECT END ERROR EVENT EXAMPLE EXCHANGE EXISTENCE EXPANSION EXPERIENCE EXPERT FACT FALL FAMILY FATHER FEAR FEELING FICTION FIELD FIGHT FIRE FLAME FLIGHT FLOWER FOLD FOOD FORCE FORM FRIEND FRONT FRUIT GLASS GOLD GOVERNMENT GRAIN GRASS GRIP GROUP GROWTH GUIDE HARBOUR HARMONY HATE HEARING HEAT HELP HISTORY HOLE HOPE HOUR HUMOUR ICE IDEA IMPULSE INCREASE INDUSTRY INK INSECT INSTRUMENT INSURANCE INTEREST INVENTION IRON JELLY JOIN JOURNEY JUDGE JUMP KICK KISS KNOWLEDGE LAND LANGUAGE LAUGH LAW LEAD LEARNING LEATHER LETTER LEVEL LIFT LIGHT LIMIT LINEN LIQUID LIST LOOK LOSS LOVE MACHINE MAN MANAGER MARK MARKET MASS MEAL MEASURE MEAT MEETING MEMORY

METAL MIDDLE MILK MIND MINE MINUTE MIST MONEY MONTH MORNING MOTHER MOTION MOUNTAIN MOVE MUSIC NAME NATION NEED NEWS NIGHT NOISE NOTE NUMBER OBSERVATION OFFER OIL OPERATION OPINION ORDER ORGANIZATION ORNAMENT OWNER PAGE PAIN PAINT PAPER PART PASTE PAYMENT PEACE PERSON PLACE PLANT PLAY PLEASURE POINT POISON POLISH PORTER POSITION POWDER POWER PRICE PRINT PROCESS PRODUCE PROFIT PROPERTY PROSE PROTEST PULL PUNISHMENT PURPOSE PUSH QUALITY QUESTION RAIN RANGE RATE RAY REACTION READING REASON RECORD REGRET RELATION RELIGION REPRESENTATIVE REQUEST RESPECT REST REWARD RHYTHM RICE RIVER ROAD ROLL ROOM RUB RULE RUN SALT SAND SCALE SCIENCE SEA SEAT SECRETARY SELECTION SELF

SENSE SERVANT SEX SHADE SHAKE SHAME SHOCK SIDE SIGN SILK SILVER SISTER SIZE SKY SLEEP SLIP SLOPE SMASH SMELL SMILE SMOKE SNEEZE SNOW SOAP SOCIETY SON SONG SORT SOUND SOUP SPACE STAGE START STATEMENT STEAM STEEL STEP STITCH STONE STOP STORY STRETCH STRUCTURE SUBSTANCE SUGAR SUGGESTION SUMMER SUPPORT SURPRISE SWIM SYSTEM TALK TASTE TAX TEACHING TENDENCY TEST THEORY THING THOUGHT THUNDER TIME TIN TOP TOUCH TRADE TRANSPORT TRICK TROUBLE TURN TWIST UNIT USE VALUE VERSE VESSEL VIEW VOICE WALK WAR WASH WASTE WATER WAVE WAX WAY WEATHER WEEK WEIGHT WIND WINE WINTER WOMAN WOOD WOOL WORD WORK WOUND WRITING YEAR

### 200 Pictured

ANGLE ANT APPLE ARCH ARM ARMY BABY BAG BALL BAND BASIN BASKET BATH BED BEE BELL BERRY BIRD BLADE BOARD BOAT BONE BOOK BOOT BOTTLE BOX BOY BRAIN BRAKE BRANCH BRICK BRIDGE BRUSH BUCKET BULB BUTTON CAKE CAMERA CARD CART CARRIAGE CAT CHAIN CHEESE CHEST CHIN CHURCH CIRCLE CLOCK CLOUD COAT COLLAR COMB CORD COW CUP CURTAIN CUSHION DOG DOOR DRAIN DRAWER DRESS DROP EAR EGG ENGINE EYE FACE FARM FEATHER FINGER FISH FLAG FLOOR FLY FOOT FORK FOWL FRAME GARDEN GIRL GLOVE GOAT GUN HAIR HAMMER HAND HAT HEAD HEART HOOK HORN HORSE HOSPITAL HOUSE ISLAND JEWEL KETTLE KEY

KNEE KNIFE KNOT LEAF LEG LIBRARY LINE LIP LOCK MAP MATCH MONKEY MOON MOUTH MUSCLE NAIL NECK NEEDLE NERVE NET NOSE NUT OFFICE ORANGE OVEN PARCEL PEN PENCIL PICTURE PIG PIN PIPE PLANE PLATE PLOUGH POCKET POT POTATO PRISON PUMP RAIL RAT RECEIPT RING ROD ROOF ROOT SAIL SCHOOL SCISSORS SCREW SEED SHEEP SHELF SHIP SHIRT SHOE SKIN SKIRT SNAKE SOCK SPADE SPONGE SPOON SPRING SQUARE STAMP STAR STATION STEM STICK STOCKING STOMACH STORE STREET SUN TABLE TAIL THREAD THROAT THUMB TICKET TOE TONGUE TOOTH TOWN TRAIN TRAY TREE TROUSERS UMBRELLA WALL WATCH WHEEL WHIP WHISTLE WINDOW WING WIRE WORM

## QUALITIES

### 100 General

ABLE ACID ANGRY AUTOMATIC BEAUTIFUL BLACK BOILING BRIGHT BROKEN BROWN CHEAP CHEMICAL CHIEF CLEAN CLEAR COMMON COMPLEX CONSCIOUS CUT DEEP DEPENDENT EARLY ELASTIC ELECTRIC EQUAL FAT FERTILE FIRST FIXED FLAT FREE FREQUENT FULL GENERAL GOOD GREAT GREY HANGING HAPPY HARD HEALTHY HIGH HOLLOW IMPORTANT KIND LIKE LIVING LONG MALE MARRIED MATERIAL MEDICAL MILITARY NATURAL NECESSARY NEW NORMAL OPEN PARALLEL PAST PHYSICAL POLITICAL POOR POSSIBLE PRESENT PRIVATE PROBABLE QUICK QUIET READY RED REGULAR RESPONSIBLE RIGHT ROUND SAME SECOND SEPARATE SERIOUS SHARP SMOOTH STICKY STIFF STRAIGHT STRONG SUDDEN SWEET TALL THICK TIGHT TIRED TRUE VIOLENT WAITING WARM WET WIDE WISE YELLOW YOUNG

### 50 Opposites

AWAKE BAD BENT BITTER BLUE CERTAIN COLD COMPLETE CRUEL DARK DEAD DEAR DELICATE DIFFERENT DIRTY DRY FALSE FEEBLE FEMALE FOOLISH FUTURE GREEN ILL LAST LATE LEFT LOOSE LOUD LOW MIXED NARROW OLD OPPOSITE PUBLIC ROUGH SAD SAFE SECRET SHORT SHUT SIMPLE SLOW SMALL SOFT SOLID SPECIAL STRANGE THIN WHITE WRONG

### NO 'VERBS'

IT IS POSSIBLE TO GET ALL THESE WORDS ON THE BACK OF A BIT OF NOTEPAPER BECAUSE THERE ARE NO 'VERBS' IN BASIC ENGLISH.

A WEEK OR TWO WITH THE RULES AND THE SPECIAL RECORDS GIVES COMPLETE KNOWLEDGE OF THE SYSTEM FOR READING OR WRITING

## XAMPLES OF WORD ORDER

THE CAMERA MAN WHO MADE AN ATTEMPT TO TAKE A MOVING PICTURE OF THE SOCIETY WOMEN, BEFORE THEY GOT THEIR HATS OFF, DID NOT GET OFF THE SHIP TILL HE WAS QUESTIONED BY THE POLICE.

WE WILL GIVE SIMPLE RULES TO YOU NOW.

## RULES

ADDITION OF 'S' TO THINGS WHEN THERE IS MORE THAN ONE

ENDINGS IN 'ER', 'ING', 'ED FROM 300 NAMES OF THINGS

'LY' FORMS FROM QUALITIES

DEGREE WITH 'MORE' AND 'MOST

QUESTIONS BY CHANGE OF ORDER, AND 'DO'.

FORM-CHANGES IN NAMES OF ACTS, AND 'THAT,' 'THIS, 'I,' 'HE,' 'YOU,' 'WHO', AS IN NORMAL ENGLISH

MEASURES NUMBERS DAYS, MONTHS AND THE INTERNATIONAL WORDS IN ENGLISH FORM.

THE ORTHOLOGICAL INSTITUTE
10 KING'S PARADE
CAMBRIDGE, ENGLAND

**B**ritish

**A**merican

**S**cientific

**I**nternational

**C**ommercial

*" One unlooked-for development of the hundred years between 2000 and 2100 was the way in which Basic English became in that short time the common language for use between nations. . . . By 2020 almost everyone was able to make use of Basic for talking and writing."—H. G. Wells.*

Put into Basic from *The Shape of Things to Come.*

*Printed in Great Britain by*
R. I. SEVERS, CAMBRIDGE

## TO THE READER

Basic English is a simple form of English which may be used as an international language or as the first step to normal English. The 850 words which are all it makes use of are printed on the folded paper at the front of the book; the rules for their operation are given in *The ABC of Basic English*; and in *Basic Step by Step* the words and structure are grouped into thirty steps for teaching purposes. Other books in and about Basic are listed at the back.

The present book is in Basic English, but, unlike the others put out in the same form, it is not specially designed for those interested in Basic as a new language. It is for use in English schools, and is chiefly important from a Basic point of view as an example of the value in education of the general idea on which the system is based. It may well, however, be of help to Basic teachers in other countries, as offering suggestions for the first stage in the teaching of those who have to have training in the Roman letters before going on to *Step by Step*.

The material here given is the outcome of long experience in teaching reading and writing to small boys and girls, and though the system worked out by Mrs. Walpole is new, it is so clearly based on common sense that no argument will be needed to make even the least expert conscious of its value. The connection between the first steps in reading and writing and Basic English, however, may not be quite so clear. Here is Mrs. Walpole's account of her reasons for using the Basic word-list as the framework of her teaching.

"A bright boy or girl of three to four years has a great number of words in his head, but his power of putting his thoughts into language is commonly very small. For one thing, there is a tendency for the words or word-groups which are stamped on his memory to be limited to certain experiences. For example, though he may have ready to his tongue a great number of names of playthings, he will be quite at a loss when it is necessary for him to give an account of something which is new to him, because he has not enough general words which may be used for all purposes. Again, his control of the words he has is frequently poor; he is not certain enough of their senses and the different ways in which they may be put together.

The great need in the first school years is for a limited selection of words which will give the young learner at the same time an instrument of which he is able to get complete control for present needs, and a framework for his increasing knowledge.

This is where Basic English comes in. The boy or girl has little trouble in getting control of the five-sixths of the Basic list which is at his level, and when he has done so he is in a position to put into words whatever he has in mind. With this as a starting point, it is possible to make quite clear to him the sense and use of more complex words. Further, he is able himself to put new ideas into simple language, and so make them truly a part of his knowledge; and the danger of his getting into the way of using words loosely is much less. Such a process is of the greatest value for the development of reasoning power and of an outlook on language which is a help at every future stage."

The idea of teaching letters by pictures first came to Mrs. Walpole in 1924, when she was teaching at the Wisbech High School Kindergarten, and the system was roughly outlined in 1925–7, while she was at the Norwich Training College. But it was not till 1935, after using it for some time at the Kingston (Ontario) Kindergarten, that the connection was made with Basic English and the details were worked out in their present form.

Under this system the boys and girls at the Kindergarten are normally able to do straightforward reading by the time they are five or six, and some specially bright ones have even given their families a shock by reading the newspaper at four. But it is one of Mrs. Walpole's chief points that the learner is never forced to go more quickly than is natural to him, and in the opinion of the mothers and fathers, and of medical men who have taken an interest in the school, there is no question of overworking young brains. The effects of the work are clearly healthy; the rate at which the boys and girls get on keeps up their interest and gives them a belief in themselves, and their free time is much fuller and happier because of the new powers which school has given them.

In the first year, when they are three years old, the boys and girls come to the Kindergarten for only six hours a week, two hours on three mornings. This year is given to getting them used to group-work, and to training their muscles for the work of the second year, when a serious start is made at reading and writing. In the second year they come to school for ten hours a week, two hours on five mornings, and by the end of that time most of them have gone through the work in this book and are reading and writing Basic without trouble. No time-limit is put upon the work, however, and, as Mrs. Walpole says again and again in her directions to the teacher, it is most important for the learner to have complete control of the first stages before going on to the later ones. The system is based on the development of the learner's reasoning power; he goes from step to step by building on what is clear to him, and is never to be forced into putting all the weight of learning on his memory.

The signs for sounds in Parts III and IV are those of the *International Phonetic Association* as used in *A Basic Phonetic Reader*[1] and *The Sounds and Forms of Basic English.*

[1] By Professor A. Lloyd James (Nelson, 1936).

## LIST OF PAGES

### Part I



### Part II

## Part III



## Part IV

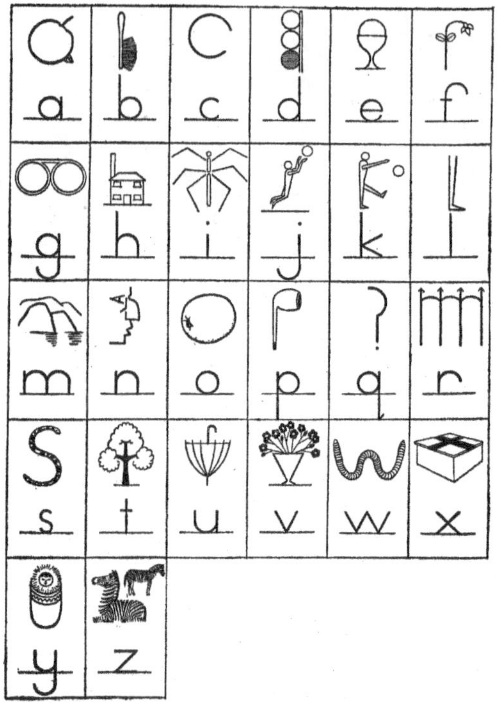
a
b
c
d
e
f
g
h
i
j
k
l
m
n
o
p
q
r
s
t
u
v
w
x
y
z

# FROM PICTURES TO LETTERS

## PART I

### A WORD TO TEACHERS

This book is an account of the special training necessary for the young boy or girl in letter-making and simple reading. Only work in connection with reading and writing is given here; training in numbers, colour, design, art, and hand-work are other very important parts of school work, but little is said about them in this book. The learning group may be of any size, from two or three to thirty or forty, but the best number is about ten. It is a good thing for those in it to be at different stages in their work, because they get much help from discussions among themselves. If the group is small, the teacher will take care that she does not get in the learners' way, and that they are not conscious of her when they are working. If the group is great in number, it is a good idea to make divisions into smaller groups for teaching.

The small boy first comes to school when he is three years old, and the first thing which has to be done is to give him the sense of being free and among friends. This is best done by the other boys, who will quickly get into the way of giving a new-comer the feeling that he is one of them. They will take him round to see the different things used in the school-room, let him see how they do their work, and have talks with him.

The special training for the first year is the development of the muscles of the hand and lower arm. Much of this year's work will have in view purposes other than reading and writing, but all hand-work is a help in this direction, because it is getting the muscles strong. In addition, to make certain that all the necessary muscles are used, and that certain forms and directions are got into the boy's mind, special work is necessary, of which an account is given in Part II of this book. It is most important for reading and writing to go forward together, and for this reason no attempt will be made at learning the letters till the muscles used in forming them have been made ready by the training given in Part II.

In the second year at school, that is, when the learner is four years old, he does his letters. These are taken in 27 steps which are given in detail in Part III. It is necessary for him to have a complete knowledge of these letters before he goes on to Part IV. It may be that Part III will be covered in two or three months; this is frequently so, and if the teacher is certain that the work has been well done, then it is time to go on to Part IV. These two Parts may be done in a year, and the boy or girl of five years will then be ready to go on to more complex sounds and reading, and at six will be able to do reading of any sort without trouble.

This is the rate of learning for the normal boy or girl under normal conditions, coming to school for not more than two hours in the morning. But take care not to let the work be controlled by the idea of getting to a given point in a given time. It is most important for the teacher not to make any attempt to go more quickly than the learner's powers will let him. It is necessary for the learner to get an idea clearly into his head before he does anything with it.

## APPARATUS

**NOTE**

The apparatus kept in the school-room is of two different sorts. There is the "general apparatus"; this is material which may be put to a number of uses, and used an unlimited number of times. Then there is the "special apparatus," for use only in the teaching of reading and writing.

All the apparatus is best kept on shelves or in drawers where the boys and girls are able to get at it themselves. In this way they will be trained in the feeling that they are responsible for it and that it is the common property of the group. When they are not working with the teacher, they will be free to take out general apparatus at any time, and when they have no more use for it they will put it back in its place in the same condition as when they took it. Putting away apparatus is a very important part of the training of the young learner. Sometimes one boy may have a desire to make an exchange of apparatus with another. He may do so if the other boy is ready to make the exchange; but when their play is over they will give the things back to one another to put away. This is the only way of keeping apparatus in order among young boys and girls. They are only able to keep in mind the place from which their work came, and they do not see where everything is kept.

Till they have been about two years at school they will not take out more than the one bit of apparatus needed at the time. When it is necessary to make use of more than one bit of apparatus in one step, as in learning some of the letters, let every bit be given out when the time comes for it and given back when it is no longer needed. The distribution may be made by one or two of the boys (though no directions for this are given in the examples), or every boy may get his things for himself.

Much attention has to be given to training in the care of apparatus. The first two things for the learners to get in mind are: (a) that the apparatus is the common property of them all; (b) that, this being so, they are all responsible for taking care of it. Small boys have a great love of putting things in order and getting them in groups. This is a good thing, because it is a help in number work. But the teacher will have to take care that the boy does not get the feeling that the pasted picture-books, dry flowers, and so on, which he has put together are his private property. They are the property of the group, and his only reward is the respect of his friends.

The apparatus has to be kept clean and new-looking. It is hard for anyone to be interested in keeping in good order things which are old and dirty. It is best, as far as possible, to have much apparatus which may be washed.

The teacher will take care that the boxes in which the apparatus is kept are strong, and not hard for small boys to get open. Boxes made of wood with covers fixed on at one side by metal joins are the best, and they may be painted in bright colours.

The "special apparatus" is best kept in a separate drawer and used only under the teacher's direction. If this is not done the small boy may get the letters mixed in his mind; and it is very important for him never to get even one wrong idea about them. A wrong idea fixed in the mind of a young boy is very hard to put right, to say nothing of the shock the discovery of the error gives to his belief in himself.

It is important to make clear to him that the learning of reading and writing is a serious business, so that he will give all his mind to it. Let him have the feeling that he is working for a purpose, an *important* purpose: he is learning to do reading and writing.

Though the special apparatus is kept in a separate drawer from the rest, it equally will be in the boys' care, and they will make the distribution of it to the group.

The letter-squares will not be kept with the special apparatus, but be in use all the time, with the general apparatus.

### GENERAL APPARATUS

This is not a complete list of general apparatus. It gives only the smallest amount with which the training of a small boy or girl may be undertaken. Almost any apparatus which gives work for the hands or eyes of the young learner is of value, and the teacher will be able to make her selection of additions to this list. Among the things needed are a number which are not on the market, and which every teacher will have to make herself.

Wherever necessary, full directions are given, and it is important, specially in connection with reading and writing, to keep to the sizes and colours here noted, which are the outcome of long observation and experiment.

Let the school-room be light and full of colour. Keep it warm, because the boys will be doing much of their work without moving about, but have the windows open as much as possible because small boys become very hard to keep under control if the air in the room is poor in quality. It is a good idea to have the walls and the top of the room very light blue, or very light yellow-brown. The brighter colours go well against these shades. The tables, seats, shelves, drawers, and boxes for apparatus may be bright reds, greens, yellows, and blues. Have all these colours in the school-room; small boys have a great love of bright colours and it is good for them to be able to see them all round them.

1. *Blackboards.* The boys' blackboard will be in the form of a band two feet wide running round three sides of the room and low enough for them to make use of without stretching. It will have a very

narrow shelf at its base for chalk, and, at spaces of two feet, hooks for dusters.

The teacher will have a separate blackboard. This will be much greater in size and further from the floor. It will be on the fourth side of the room.

2. *Seats and Tables.* The seats and tables are to be of wood, very strongly made and painted in bright colours. Have the seats the right size for small boys, and such that they are able to take them from place to place. The tables will be of a size for four boys to do their work at in comfort, and of a weight which may be lifted without trouble by two boys. It is necessary for training in the moving of seats and tables to be given and for all errors to be pointed out. To take up a seat, the boy gets at the back of it and puts his hands on the two sides ; he then takes it up and goes off with it. To take up a table, two boys are needed, one at one end and one at the other ; they put their hands under it and take it up, one boy facing the direction in which they are going, the other walking back.

The teacher will have a special seat and table, greater in size than those of the boys.

3. *Shelves and Drawers.* Have the shelves and drawers of wood, and bright in colour. It is important to have them low enough, so that they are not out of the boys' range, and for all the drawers to go in and out without trouble.

4. *Phonograph.* It is necessary to have a phonograph and, if possible, a piano. A great number of records of widely different sorts will be needed. With training, the boys will be able to put the phonograph on themselves. They will, in addition, quickly be able to make very simple music, like a simple scale, on the piano.

5. *Paper.* Paper is very important in the school-room. It is, roughly, of two sorts: white for letter-making, and coloured for picture-making, cutting out, and hand-work.

Much paper will be needed, and it is a good idea to have a 'paper-shelf' or 'paper-drawer' where it is kept. The teacher will take care that there is at all times paper of different sorts and sizes on this shelf. Never give the boys the idea that there is a limited amount of paper, but do not let them put any paper which is not fully used into the waste-paper-basket.

The coloured paper is of two sorts, rough and smooth. The rough will take chalk, and may in addition be used for cutting and pasting. The smooth will not take chalk, and so, though it is beautiful for cutting and pasting, it is of no use for picture-making.

The white paper is of two sorts, lined and unlined. The lined paper is used only for the work in Part IV. Till that stage the boy will make his ' base-line ' himself with a measuring rule. Only white paper will be used for letter-making.

6. *Chalk.* There are two sorts of chalk: thick, for use on the blackboards, and a softer chalk for use on paper. Do not let these chalks get mixed; the soft chalks are not for use on the blackboard, and the thick chalk is not for use on the paper. The blackboard chalk will be kept on the little shelf under the wall blackboards, the paper chalks in boxes on another shelf.

Let the two sorts be as bright and of as wide a range of colours as possible.

7. *Pencils.* The pencils will be kept in a box. Get them with soft lead, and,

if possible, painted in bright colours. It is best for them to have a rubber at the end, so that the boys may be trained to make use of this for rubbing out any wrong lines they make. This is of great value in letter-making. The boy sees the right form of the letter, then he takes a look at the one he has made and puts his errors right with the help of the rubber.

The pencils will be kept sharp by the boys themselves with a machine.

8. *Rulers.* The rulers are used to make straight lines, and later in number work.

9. *Plasticine.* Plasticine has a great number of uses and a great amount of it will be needed. It is important for the boys to be expert at making a good round ball of Plasticine. This is the first step in all Plasticine work.

10. *Scissors.* Scissors will have round, not pointed, ends.

11. *Paste.* Paste is needed for pasting paper.

12. *Coloured Balls.* These are small, brightly-coloured balls of wood, with a hole through the middle, so that they may be threaded on cords. They are of great use in number work and design.

13. *Coloured Markers.* These are small rounds of coloured cardboard, again for number and design work.

14. *Sticks.* The sticks are of different sizes and colours. They are for use in picture-making, design, and number work. Putting them in order is very good training for small fingers.

15. *Printing Sticks and Paint.* The printing sticks have ends of different sorts, square, round, and star-formed. These ends are covered with paint and their forms are then printed on paper. In this way different designs may be made. This is good training in the control of the hands.

16. *Bricks.* There will be a great number of bricks, of different sizes, forms, and colours. The letter bricks, though listed among the special apparatus and kept in a separate box, are put with the general apparatus and used at any time.

17. *Picture Makers.*[1] These are seven little Bakelite forms, from which, by putting them in different positions and groups, a number of pictures may be made.

[1] These may be had from The Orthological Institute, 10, King's Parade, Cambridge, England, at the price of 1/-, post free.

18. *Cardboard Forms.* Cardboard forms of a number of things will be needed—simple forms, like squares and circles, and more complex forms, like boys and girls, trees, houses, and so on. These are to give help in picture-making and muscle control; the boy puts the cardboard form on paper and makes a line round it with a pencil. They will not be greatly used after the first year or so, and the teacher will take care that this apparatus does not put a stop to free-hand picture-making.

19. *Finger Paints.* Finger paints have a great number of uses in the school-room. Their value is unlimited and it is well to make use of them whenever possible.

20. *Automatic Playthings.* Automatic playthings are of great use. It is important for them to be strong, and made in such a way that the boys are able to take them to bits and put them together again.

21. *Pasted Picture Books.* A number of books with unlined paper will be kept, and pictures from old newspapers and books cut out and pasted in them by the boys. These may sometimes be grouped in a special order, sometimes not.

22. *Books.* A great number of books will be kept on shelves for the use of the

boys and girls. They may be picture-books, or books having simple reading-material with pictures.

The teacher's books will be kept on a separate shelf. They will be story, verse, and song books.

In addition to this material there will be other apparatus made by the teacher for special purposes, such as putting together colours and forms in their right orders.

### SPECIAL APPARATUS

1. *The Wall Picture-Letters.* These are cards with the letters and their pictures on them, to be put on the wall in a line from A to Z. The designs for the letters and pictures are given separately in Part III and together at the front of the book.

Put every letter and its picture on a separate light blue card, so that they may be taken down and used one by one. A darker blue band of cardboard or thick paper is first fixed on the wall, and the wall picture-letters are put on this with pins.

On the lower half of the card is the letter, on the top half the picture which goes with it. The pictures may be coloured, but it is important for the letters to be black. The best size for the cards is 12 inches by 6 inches, with the letters based on parts of a 2-inch circle. Make all the lines but the floor line, which is narrower, ¼-inch wide.

2. *The Lettered Bricks*. These are of solid wood with six equal sides 1½ inches square. On the six sides of every brick are : a letter in three different forms, its picture, a number, and a round black mark. For example, the first brick has on one side the letter ' a ' in writing, on another a printed ' a,' on another a great A, on another a coloured picture of an apple, on another the number 1, and on the side opposite to this a round mark. The second brick gives the letter ' b ' with the number 2, the third the letter ' c ' with the number 3, and so on through all the letters. The numbers are given only up to 10, the

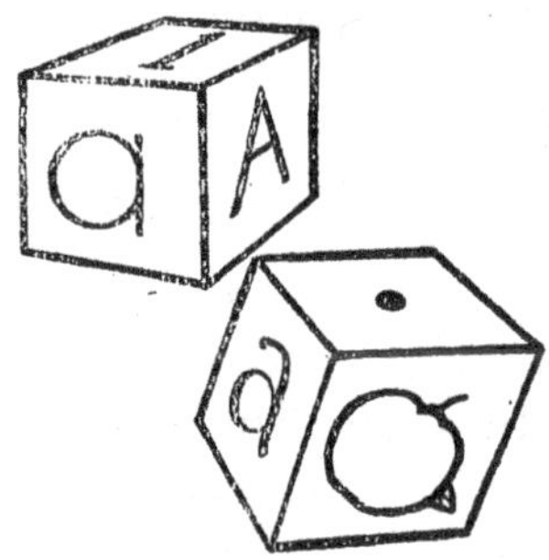

letter ' k,' for example, having 1 again, the letter ' l ', 2, and so on.

Two complete groups of these bricks will be in use all the time.

3. *The Letter-Makers.* These are 13 parts of letters cut out in black card: circles, half-circles, and sticks of different sizes. The boys are given a white card with a black floor-line, and have to put the parts together on this to make the different letters.

The sticks are marked with a round black mark for every inch. For example, the smallest has one round mark on it, and the longest has four. This is not only of use when the teacher is giving directions; it gives the boys the idea of the relations between the sizes of the different sticks.

These forms are best kept in strong paper covers. There are:

One 4-inch stick
One 3-inch stick
Four 2-inch sticks
Two 1-inch sticks
One complete circle, 2 inches across
Two ¾ circles, 2 inches across
Two ½ circles, 2 inches across.

These Letter-Makers are of great value in helping the learner to see the form of the letter before he makes any attempt to put it into writing. They may further be used, under the direction of the teacher, to put right a wrong idea, or to give help to a boy who is not certain.

4. *Letter Squares.* The letter squares are $\frac{1}{2}$-inch squares of white cardboard. Every one has on it a printed letter, so that they may be put together on the table to make words. These are a great help in word-building Keep them in paper covers.

5. *Reading-Cards.* These are needed when the letters are gone over a second time. Their use is made clear in Part IV, and the material to be put on them is given at the end of it. Make the cards of light blue cardboard with the new words at the top printed in red and the rest in black.

6. *Word-Lists.* These, again, are for use in connection with Part IV, and one for every day is given at the end of the book. They are lists of words having in them the letter which is being taken on any given day, printed in black on light blue cards.

7. *Wall Learning-Words.* When a harder word is taken, it is a good idea for the

teacher to put it into a statement and put the statement up on the wall. Let the writing be of a size which may be seen with comfort from any part of the room.

A further help is to make pictures to go with these statements.

8. *Wall Verse.* Verses put up on the wall are of use for keeping examples of good writing before the boys. It is best to take verses of which they have knowledge, and, again, take care that the writing is of a size to be readily made out.

9. *Great Letters.* When the great letters are gone over a second time, it is a good idea for the teacher to put up a wall card with them on it, formed as clearly and beautifully as possible. This is a great help in getting the forms of these letters into the boys' minds.

# PART II

## MUSCLE TRAINING

The three-year-old boy has little control over his hands, and much time and care have to be given at first to the development of the muscles of the hands and lower arms, with a view to the writing he will do later.

After a year of this first stage of training he is ready to make his letters with his pencil without feeling that it is hard work. He is able to give all his mind to the business of reading and writing, because he is not troubled with the development of unused muscles.

This muscle-training is done step by step, and a selection has been made of such simple operations as will be of interest to small boys and girls. A great number of these are done in the form of play guided by the teacher. At other times the teacher lets the boys and girls make free use of the apparatus, without help of any sort.

## DANCING TO MUSIC

The first thing necessary is to get all the muscles of the body working freely, and one of the best ways of doing this is by dancing to music. A record is played on the phonograph, and in a short time the boys take pleasure in moving their feet, hands, and bodies in harmony with the music. After a time they get the feeling of the rhythm and are no longer self-conscious, every boy moving round freely with the music guiding his motions.

No complex or uncommon motion is made at first, the only muscles moved being those which are used in normal everyday acts, such as the muscles of the neck, the hands, the legs, and the feet.

This dancing to music has another effect, in addition to its use in the development of the muscles; it takes away the self-conscious feeling of the new boy, giving him a belief in his power to do things and making everything seem less strange. It is part of the school work for all the first year, the teacher taking care that all the muscles in turn are given a chance of development. It may be that some music will go well with motions of the arms only, other music with motions of the head, and so on.

## ARM MOTIONS

Special training of the arm muscles, in the form of play, is started at the same time as dancing. These arm motions are done every morning before any apparatus is given out. It takes two or three weeks for the boys and girls to get used to a new motion so that they are able to do it naturally and without trouble.

The old motions are done every day in addition to any new attempt, so that after two or three months a short time will first be given to learning the new motion, and then all those which have been done before will be gone through very quickly.

The first step in all muscle development is to get the muscles soft and loose before giving them work, and the teacher will make certain that the boys are taking in deep regular breaths. There are a number of ways of making this seem like play. Six suggestions are made in the material given, and, guided by these, any teacher will be able to make others.

When the boys are completely at rest, they may do the arm motions. These are done slowly at first, then more and more quickly when the arms get more under control. They are done loosely and freely at the start, then with the arms stiff, then with the arms stiff using only the lower arm, then with one arm after the other. After that the hand is moved, and then the fingers. Lastly the arms, going round separately, are moved freely and quickly.

These motions are the first things done by the boys and girls every morning, when they are bright and rested, and ready for hard work.

They are kept up for not more than five or six minutes.

### EXAMPLE 1

**The up and down motion, front**

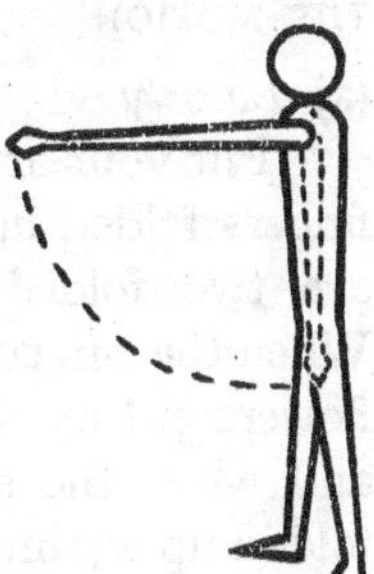

" Boys and girls, go to a place in the room where you will have enough space to put out your arms freely."

BREATHING

" We are going to get a paper bag full of air.

Put your hands to your mouth as if they were round a bag, blowing hard into them. Keep on till the bag is full.

Now let your hands come suddenly together over the bag, and it will go off with a burst."

GETTING LOOSE

" Keep your eyes shut and say to yourself that you are a soft cloth-baby. Your inside is of soft wool and you are not strong enough to keep upright.

Let your arms and legs and body go loose and your head be hanging down in front.

Take in a great breath through your nose and let it out again through your mouth ; you are a very sad cloth-baby."

THE MOTION

(a) *Loosely*

" Put your arms out in front, with your fingers folded in your hands. Your hands are two folded flowers on their stems. When the sun comes up in the morning the flowers put up their heads and come open, and when the sun goes to bed they are folded up again.

The sun is coming. Up go the flowers on their stems, high up over your head. Now it is day. Let the flowers come open. Now the sun is going to bed. Get your flowers shut up again and let your arms come slowly down.

Do this again, first with one arm and then with the other."

(b) *With arms stiff*

"We are going to be a lift. The lift is in a great tall building and its work is to take persons up and down from floor to floor. Your two arms are the lift, the lowest floor is down by your sides and the top floor is high up over your head. Keep your arms straight and make them go up to the top of the building. Coming down we make a stop to let someone get in. Then down we all go to the lowest floor. Someone gets in and we take him up to the fourth floor. Another person on the top floor has given the bell a push. Up we go to get him, etc.

Now see if we are able to make the lift go with one arm, etc."

(c) *The lower arm motions*

"Now we are in a lift in a smaller building. Keep the top part of your arms by your sides and let only the lower part go.

All make the smaller lift go up and down.

Now see if you are able to make it go first with one arm and then with the other."

(d) *Hand motions*

" Now this is an even smaller lift. Only your hands are to be used. Put your arms out straight in front and let your hands go up and down, taking persons from floor to floor."

(e) *Finger motions*

" Go to your seats. See how I make music on the piano. I give the little black and white notes touches with my fingers and they make the music.

Keep your eyes shut and let your table be a piano. While I make music on my piano you do the same on yours. Give little touches on the table with your fingers."

(f) *Free motions*

" Get up on your feet. We are going to make music with the bells in the top of the church. The bells are fixed onto long cords, and when we give the cords a pull the bells will be sounded.

We all have the ends of two bell-cords, one in one hand and one in the other, and we are going to give them a pull in turn.

'Ding dong, ding dong,' say the bells, and we will make a song in rhythm with the pulls."

They have a simple little song to go with this motion. "Ding dong, ding dong, ding dong, ding dong," down the music scale.

## EXAMPLE 2

### The up and down motion with arms out to the sides

BREATHING

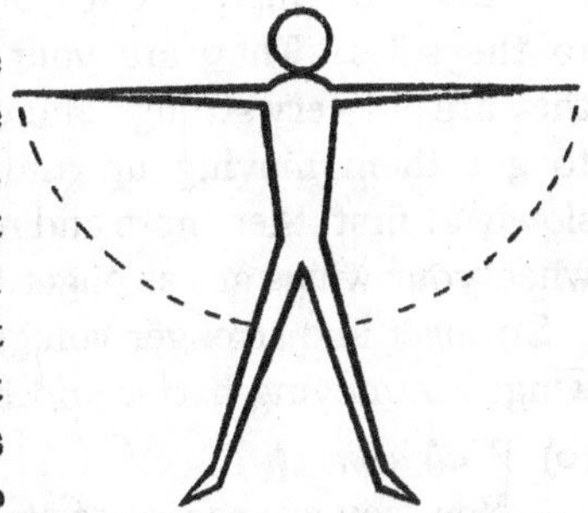

"You are going to be the wind. Send out your breath with great force to get the clouds moving. Go running round the room blowing hard to make the clouds go quicker."

GETTING LOOSE

"Go to a place in the room where there is enough space to put out your arms freely. Get well balanced, with your feet a little parted. You are a horse who has come a long, long journey. He is so tired that he is not able to make another move. He is so tired that he is not able even to get down on the floor.

Let your head go forward and keep your eyes shut. The horse is so tired that he goes to sleep on his feet."

THE MOTION

(a) *Loosely*

"We are going to be little birds attempting their first flight. Put your arms out to the sides. They are your wings, and they are not very strong. Make an attempt to get them moving up and down. Go slowly at first, then more and more quickly when your wings get stronger.

Stronger and stronger you get, and your wings are moving better and better."

(b) *With arms stiff*

"Now you are the great strong King of birds, able to go high up over the clouds. Keep your arms quite straight and make them go in great slow motions from your sides out and up to the top of your head.

Now go more quickly. Keep your eyes shut and see in your mind the land and the sea far under you."

(c) *Lower arm motions*

"Now you are a smaller bird. Your wings are smaller, so keep the top parts of your arms by your sides and make only the lower parts go up and down.

Now do the same with your hands only.

See if you are able to make a flight with one wing broken. Keep the broken wing by your side, etc."

(d) *Free motions*

"The fowls on a farm have wings, but they are not able to get far up in the air with them. When they are running round quickly, they are helped by their wings.

All go running round with your arms out for wings. Make the noise which fowls make, and let your arms go up and down to give you help in your running.

Go to your seats."

(e) *Finger motions*

"You have a writing-machine in front of you on the table. By giving a touch to the little letter buttons you will make the machine do writing.

You are writing a letter to your mother; make your fingers go up and down giving little touches to the buttons."

## EXAMPLE 3

### The side to front motion

BREATHING

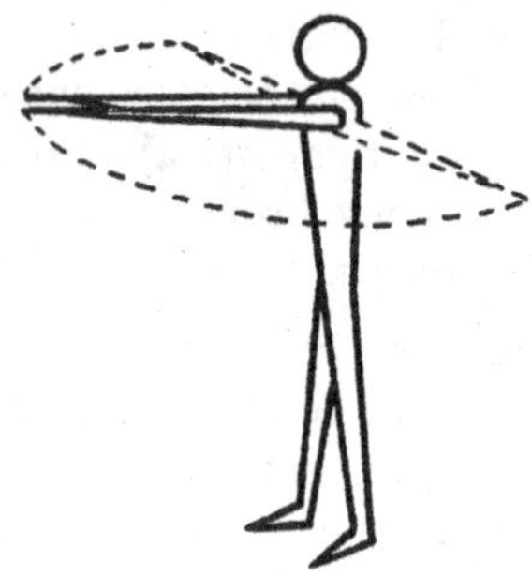

" Everyone take a seat on the floor with one leg across the other. Keep your eyes shut and say to yourself that you have a basin between your legs. The basin is full of water and soap. You have a pipe, and with the pipe you are going to make air-balls of the soap and water.

Get a little water in the pipe, and take in a great breath. Now let your breath go slowly, with great care, through the pipe. You are making a beautiful brightly coloured air-ball. Send your breath out slowly, because if you send it out quickly the air-ball will be broken. Now give the pipe a little shake and the air-ball will go sailing up into the room.

Make two or three more air-balls.

Now get on your feet and go round the

room keeping the air-balls up in the air with your breath."

GETTING LOOSE

"Go to a place in the room where you will have enough space to put out your arms. Get well balanced on your feet, put your arms out, and keep your eyes shut. You are a snow-man.

Now the sun comes out and gets warmer and warmer. You become softer and softer, and part of you becomes water. Let your arms come down slowly while more and more of you is being turned into water. Let your head go forward. Your arms and legs and body are getting bent and going soft and loose. In a short time you will be completely turned into water."

THE MOTION

(a) *Loosely*

"Put your feet together and your arms out straight to the sides. Put your arms almost together in front, then out again. Do this three or four times."

(b) *With arms stiff*

"Your arms are scissors and they come together, making cuts. Get your arms open and shut like scissors."

(c) *Lower arm motions*

"This time make the scissors go completely across one another."

(d) *Free motions*

"Let your arms have a rest for a minute. Now you are a man who has been driving horses on a cold morning. His hands are very cold and he gets them warm by sending his arms across one another and giving sharp blows to the sides of his body. Do this a number of times hard enough to get your cold hands warm again."

(e) *Finger motions*

"Get down on your knees and keep your eyes shut. You are on the grass by the side of a little running river. The fall wind has sent beautiful coloured leaves into the water and they are being taken down by the current.

Put your hand into the water and take out a leaf. Put it in with your fingers wide open and then let them come together. Now put the leaf on the grass and give your hand a shake to get it dry.

Put in the other hand and take out a leaf in the same way."

## EXAMPLE 4

### The side to side motion

BREATHING

" Put out your hand as if it had a flower in it.

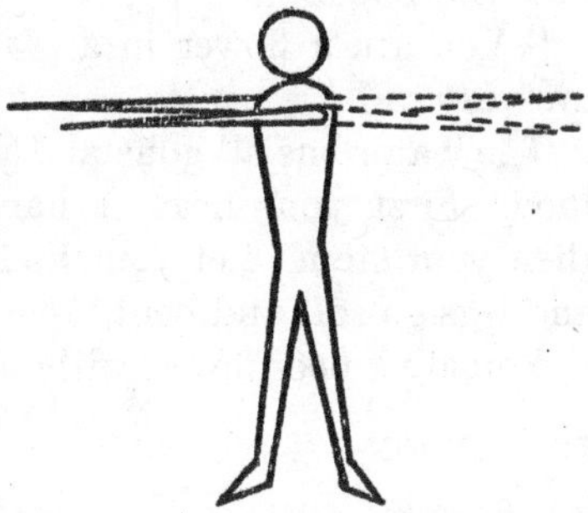

Take a look at the flower.

It is a ' clock ' flower. It is a great ball of soft white feathers. By blowing on it we may make some of them go sailing off into the air.

Go on blowing till all the feathers have gone.

What number of blows did you have to give before all the feathers were gone?"

" I gave seven blows."

" Then it is seven by the clock. Now you see why we say it is a ' clock ' flower.

Take another flower and see what the time is again. It may be different this time.

Naturally, this way of getting the time

is only in play, and is not serious. To get the true time we take a look at a clock."

GETTING LOOSE

" You are a flower in a glass, but you are very sad.

The water has all gone and you have no food. First your head is hanging down, then your stem. Let your body and arms and legs go soft and bent.

You are a poor flower without water."

THE MOTION

(a) *Loosely*

" Go to a place in the room where you have enough space to put out your arms freely.

Put them out straight in front. Now let them go from one side to the other. They are two persons walking on a road one after the other. When the first one gets to the end they make a turn and go back, so that the one who was at the back is now in front.

Do this three or four times. Then let your arms come to rest by your sides."

(b) *With arms stiff*

" Your body is the upright support of a door. Your arms are the door.

Put them out, and let them go forward and back like a door on its support.

Keep your arms very straight. Now let them come to rest at your sides."

(c) *Lower arm motions*

" You are a tree in the wind.

Put up your arms for branches. Let the tops of the branches, the lower parts of your arms, go back and forward in the wind."

(d) *Hand motions*

" Now the wind is less strong and only your leaves are moving. Keep your arms at rest, and let your hands make side to side motions."

(e) *Finger motions*

" You are a little woodman making music on his pipe. He puts the small pipe to his mouth, and while blowing through it keeps his fingers going over the different holes in the pipe.

I will put a record on the phonograph, and you go dancing round making music on your pipe. Keep in mind that the best music comes from the pipes whose fingers do the hardest work."

## EXAMPLE 5

**Round and round with arms out to the sides**

BREATHING

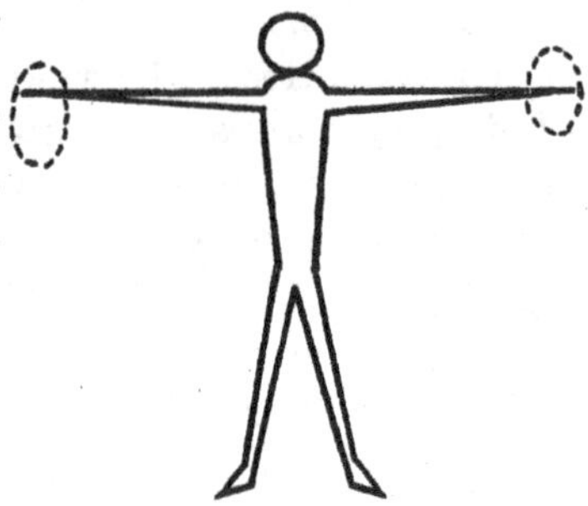

"Get down on your knees and we will make a fire in play.

Get some paper, put the sticks on one by one, and then put the coal on top of them.

Now get a match and put a light to the fire. The fire still does not go very well. We will give it a blow with our breath.

Go on blowing harder and harder till it is burning and the flames and smoke come up."

GETTING LOOSE

" Get on your feet and let us be very tired for a minute.

Let's be little black boys in a warm land.

All day we have had great weights of cotton on our backs.

The sun is very, very warm and sends his great rays down on us.

Let us be so tired that we are unable to go to bed. Keep your head and arms hanging down and your eyes shut.

Take in a deep, deep breath."

THE MOTION

(a) *Loosely*

" Put your arms out straight.

Now send them round in great circles.

You are the two great wheels under the back of a ship which take it forward.

You are under water and the waves come over you."

(b) *With arms stiff*

" Now you are the wheels of a train, round and round you go, stiffly and quickly."

(c) *Lower arm motion*

" Now you are the wheels of a small train, a plaything.

Let only the lower parts of your arms go round.

Let your arms come to rest by your sides.

Now go to your seats."

(d) *Hand motions*

" Put your bent arms on the table with the hands pointing up.

Now keep your arms stiff and make your hands go round in circles.

Do this a number of times; then let every finger in turn make an attempt at moving in a circle while the other part of the hand is at rest."

(e) *Free motions*

"Get on your feet and let your arms be the great wood sails of a grain-crushing machine.

The wind comes and sends them round and round in great circles.

Round and round go your arms in great wide circles, one after the other."

### EXAMPLE 6

### Round and round in front

BREATHING

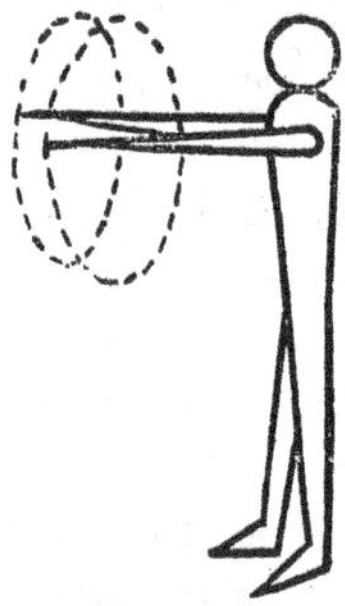

"For our breathing today we are going to be the wind over the sea. The wind sees a ship with all its sails up, and he goes to send it forward. Take in a great breath and let it out in a great blow. Do it again and again, getting stronger and stronger. On and on the ship goes till it comes at last to the land. Then it puts down its sails and the wind's work is ended."

GETTING LOOSE

" We are going to make ourselves tired and then come to rest by picturing a flag.

Put out your arms and let them go back and forward like a flag in the wind.

Now there is no wind and your flag goes down. Your arms go down to your sides.

There comes a little soft wind and you make a small motion.

Again there is no wind, and your arms come to rest. Your flag is hanging down in folds."

THE MOTION

" Go to a place in the room where you are able to put out your arms freely.

We are going to make great circles with our arms."

(a) *Loosely*

" Put your arms out in front and let them go round in great circles."

(b) *With arms stiff*

" Now we will make our arms go round like two great wheels. Keep them stiff and let them go round together in the same direction.

Now let them go in different directions.

Let your arms come to rest at your sides."

(c) *Lower arm motion*

"Now let only the lower parts of your arms go round. They are smaller wheels."

(d) *Hand motions*

"Go back to your seats and put your bent arms on the table with your hands pointing up. Let only your hands go round in circles."

(e) *Finger motions*

"Let your hands be insects and your fingers insects' legs. Send your hands walking over the table by taking little steps with the fingers. Let the insects go on, over the tables, down to the floor, and up the walls as high as your hands will go."

(f) *Free motions*

"Do the twisting motion of making wool into a ball."

## THE USE OF THE PENCIL

Special training in the use of the pencil has to be given every day in the first school year, to get the hands ready for learning writing. In this way the small boy gets control of his pencil and is able to make circles and straight lines without trouble. This teaching is given in the form of play, but the teacher will take care that it is regular and complete.

The first attempts are made at the blackboard with chalk. When the boy has an idea of what he is doing, and some control of his arm muscles, he is given paper and chalk. When he is able to make use of this without trouble he is given paper and pencil. This is not to say that the small boy is not to have a pencil till he is at the stage where he will have complete control of it. He is to be free at all times to make the selection of his apparatus, but the teacher will take him through these steps in addition to his other work. It is a good idea, if the group is not very small, to take one or two boys in turn and go through the steps given here. These steps may be taken in any order. Some suggestions are made for turning them into play, and with these as examples, others will readily come to mind.

This training gets the boy of four years to a point where he is ready to give all his mind to the business of learning and writing his letters, untroubled by the control of his pencil or by tired muscles.

1. THE CIRCLE

The circle is best taken in one direction, from right to left. When an outline circle is made—that is, one which has no lines inside it—the join will come at the middle of the right side.

(a) A Corkscrew Circle

1. *From the inside out*

Make a start in the middle with a round mark. Go round and round, never taking the chalk off, and getting greater and greater.

Suggestions for play: A woman making a ball of wool. When the ball is done, put some needles into it.

2. *From the outside in*

Make a start at the right-hand edge and go round first in a great circle, then, keeping the chalk on, round and round inside that, getting smaller and smaller till you get to the middle.

Suggestions for play: Making a picture of an orange and colouring it.

(b) An Outline Circle

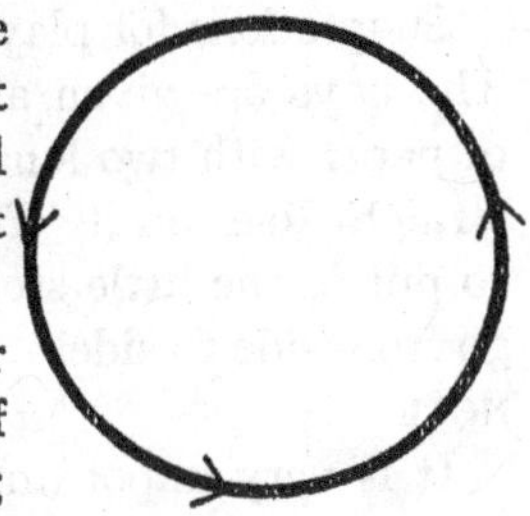

These may be made in all sizes, but with the join at all times on the right side.

Suggestions for play: A box full of oranges or apples; air balls going round; play balls in the air; wheels; etc.

2. THE STRAIGHT LINE

(a) *Up and down*

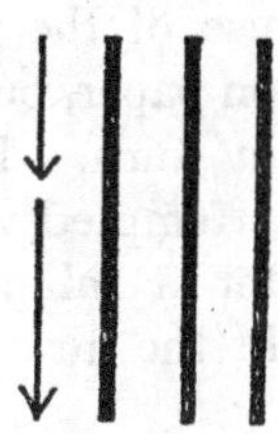

These are all to be made from the top down, and it is best to have a floor-line to keep them level.

Sometimes they will be tall, sometimes short, but it is best to make lines of them of the same size.

Suggestions for play: Grass in a field; a line of men going to work.

(b) *From side to side*

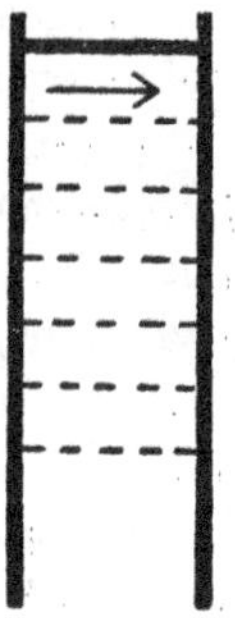

These are all made in one direction—from left to right.

Suggestions for play: Steps. The boys are given a long bit of paper with two long parallel straight lines on it. They have to put in the little steps which go from side to side.

NOTE

It is very important for the two hands to get equal training. Let everything be done first with two hands together on the blackboard; then with one hand; then the other. It is not possible to make use of the two hands at the same time on paper, but take care that they are used in turn. Before any new operation is attempted with the chalk, it is first done for a minute or two as an arm motion in the air.

# PART III

## THE TEACHING OF THE LETTERS

### NOTE TO THE TEACHER

The teaching of the letters is given here in great detail, but it is not necessary with the group to take every one so fully. The boys and girls quickly get a knowledge of the pictures and their letters from the older ones who have gone through the first stages of the training. That is why it is so important to have the complete line of picture-letters on the wall all through the year.

After three or four letters have been taken, the learners get the idea, and when a picture has been talked about they will be able to say what the sound of the letter is. If they are not, it is a sign that there is something wrong. It may be that they have not been given enough time to get the name of the picture fixed in their minds. If they are not able to give the sound of the letter when they are questioned, it is a good idea to go over the name of the picture again. Naturally the idea of

abcde
fghijkl
mnopq
rstuvw
xyz

the picture-letters does not come to them till one or two hours teaching have been given.

The letters frequently get such a strong grip on the minds of little boys and girls that care has to be taken not to let letter-acting, letter-writing, or letter-painting have any place in their dancing or designing, or in any form of art work. It is best to let them make only simple black letters—no colours, no unnecessary lines—so that they will see clearly that letters are not things for ornament, but instruments with which work is done.

The teaching is given here in the form of talks between the group and the teacher, and this is the best way of doing it. The teacher may simply go through these talks, letting the boys give the answers to the questions. Their answers, unlike those in the examples, will probably have some errors, and will certainly at times be off the point. But by a wise direction of questions, the teacher will in time get the right answers.

It may not be necessary to go over the teaching for every letter in detail, but it *is* necessary to take the chief points for every letter. Much hand and muscle work is needed in learning and writing any letter.

In connection with every letter, the teacher will make certain that the boys get these six points well into their heads:

(1) The name of the thing in the picture.
(2) The form of the picture.
(3) The form of the letter, and the way in which it is like the picture.
(4) The name of the letter (the 'sound-name').
(5) How to make the letter, without errors and without trouble.
(6) How to put in writing words in which the letter is used.

1

## A GENERAL TALK

"Boys and girls, have a look at the line of pictures on the wall.

From them we are going to get the names of our letters, so that we will be able to do reading and writing.

This is a line of picture-letters.

Is anyone able to say which are the pictures and which are the letters?"

Some boy or girl then takes a pointer

and puts it against a picture and a letter and says which is which.

" Now will one of the older boys give us the names of all the pictures and letters?"

An older boy, or the teacher, then takes a pointer and goes through the line quickly, saying the names of the letters and their pictures in this way: **a** for apple, **b**$^{ə}$ for brush, **k**$^{ə}$ for curve, etc.

" Now let us have a good look at these picture-letters and see if we are able to give the names of some of them."

The teacher puts the pointer against ' s.'

" What is that picture?"

" It is a snake."

" Will anyone make an attempt at naming the letter?"

" It is **s**."

" Everyone say **s**-for-snake."

The teacher puts the pointer against ' W.'

" What is that picture?"

" It is a worm."

" Is anyone able to give the name of the letter?"

" It is **w**$^{ə}$."

" Everyone say **w**$^{ə}$-for-worm.

Later we will be able to say the names

of the letters without the names of the pictures, this way: **a**, **b**$^{ə}$, **k**$^{ə}$, etc.

Then we will put the letters together and make words, like this: **k**$^{ə}$**-a-t**$^{ə}$ 'cat,' and so we will be able to do reading.

All printed reading material, such as books and newspapers, is made up of letters like these.

See this newspaper: it is all covered with black words, and the words are all formed of black letters.

This book is the same. Have a look for yourselves.

All the letters are in our wall pictures. By placing them in different orders we may make words."

2

ɔ-for-orange

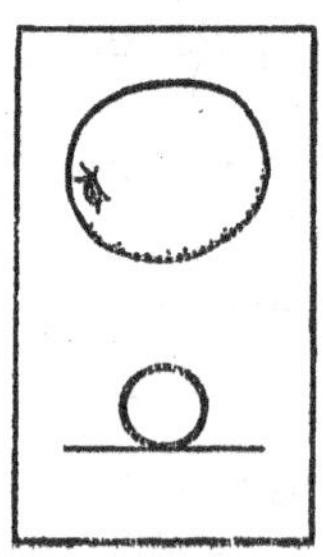

*Apparatus :*

(i) An orange.

(ii) Orange-coloured chalk; white paper.

(iii) Pencils ; round flat cardboard forms ; orange paper ; white paper ; scissors ; paste.

(iv) White paper with a line on it.

The teacher takes the wall-card 'o' and puts it face down on her table. She now takes up the orange and everyone has a look at it.

"What is this ?"

"It is an orange."

"All say the word **'ɔrindʒ** with care."

Put your hands out in front as if you had an orange in them."

Everyone makes his hands into a cup and then makes motions of rolling the orange round and round to get the feeling of something round and solid.

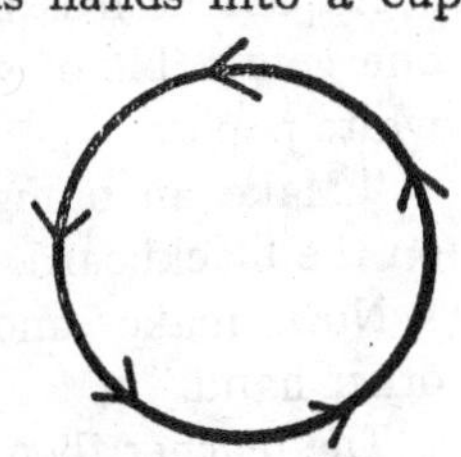

"Now put out your two hands and make the round form in the air, this way."

Everyone makes circles with his two hands three or four times.

" You are making circles."

The teacher now takes the orange-coloured chalk and makes a great circle on the blackboard, keeping the chalk moving with a screw-like motion and making smaller and smaller circles till she gets to the middle, when the great circle is full. Everyone does the same thing in the air with his two hands, first together and then separately, till the teacher is certain that they have the direction (right to left) well fixed in their minds.

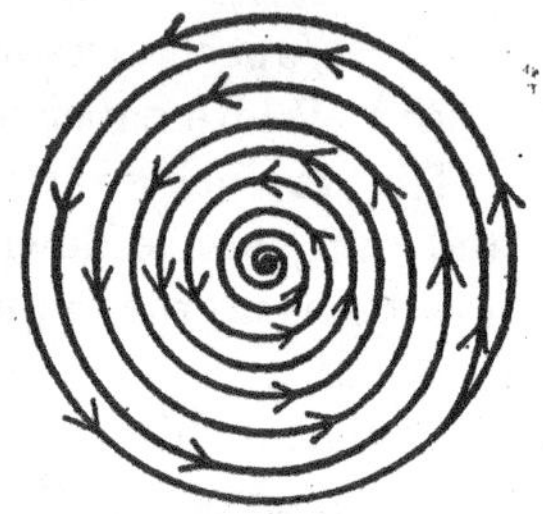

Apparatus ii is now given out. Everyone gets a bit of orange chalk and some white paper.

" Make an orange like the one I made on the blackboard.

Now make another one with your other hand."

The teacher then takes up the wall-card 'o' and puts a finger on the picture.

" This is the orange. The black thing under it is the letter. Is anyone able to give the name of the letter?"

“ It is ɔ.”

“ Everyone say ɔ with great care.

Now make a letter under your pictures. Take care to make it so that it will not be possible for me to see where you have made the join.”

The teacher has a look at everyone’s work and gives help where it is needed.

“ Now you have made ɔ-for-orange.”

Everyone in turn says “ ɔ-for-orange,” putting his finger on the letter and the picture while doing so.

“ Now on the other side of the paper make the letter with no picture. Make a number of ɔ’s all over the paper, great ones and small ones. Take care that they are all good round circles with no joins to be seen.”

The teacher goes round looking at everyone’s work and giving them help.

“ Now take a good look at your letters and see which is the most beautiful.

Make a square frame round it with your chalk and give the paper to me.”

Apparatus iii is now given out. Everyone gets a pencil, a flat round of cardboard 2 inches across, a bit of white paper of the same size and form as the wall-card, some orange-coloured paper, scissors, and paste.

" Put the round cardboard on the orange-coloured paper. Keep it from moving and make a line round it with your pencil. Take off the cardboard, and with the scissors make a cut all round the line. That is the picture of the orange. Put paste on the back and get it fixed at one end of the white paper. It is a picture of the orange like the one on the wall card.

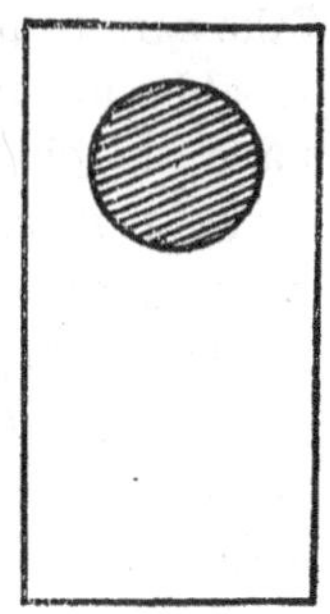

Now take the round cardboard again and put it under the picture of the orange and make a line round it. Take off the cardboard. That is the letter ɔ. Your picture is now like the wall-card ɔ-for-orange."

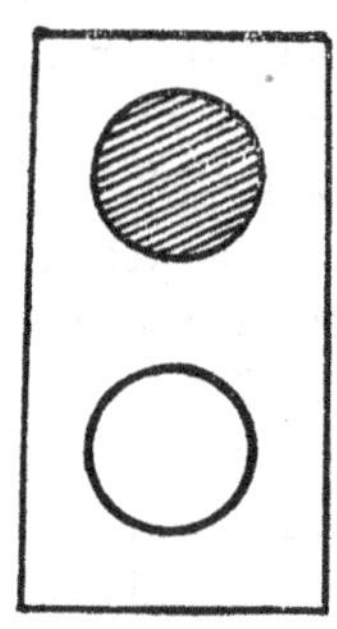

Everyone says " ɔ-for-orange," putting a finger on the letter and the picture while doing so.

" You may take this paper for Mother to see, and you will say to her that it is ɔ-for-orange."

Every boy and girl is now given a bit of white paper with one line on it.

" This line is the floor-line.

Put your finger on it and make it go from one end to the other, from the left end to the right end.

We put all the letters on a floor-line to keep them in the right positions. Some are seated on the line, some have their feet on it, and some have tails which go under it.

Letter ɔ is seated on the floor line. I will do one on the blackboard.

Now make a line of letter ɔ's on your floor-line. Make them all the same size and all seated on the line ; do not let any come jumping up off the floor-line, and do not let any go under it; and take care that not one of them has a join which may be seen."

The teacher goes round to see that the pencils are being rightly used, that the letters are being made in the right direction, and that the two hands are being used in turn.

3

## i-for-insect

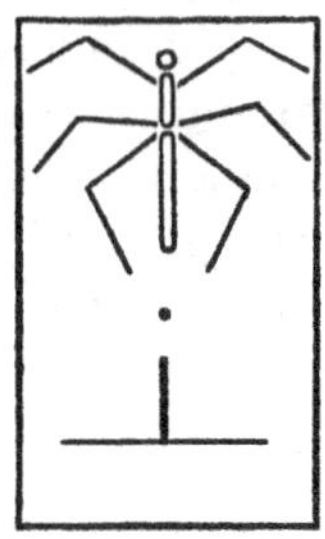

*Apparatus :*

(i) Pictures of insects.

(ii) Sticks and small round markers.

(iii) Pencils, white paper, and rulers.

The teacher takes down the wall-card 'i' and puts it before the group. She puts her finger on the picture.

"What is this animal?"

"It is an insect."

The teacher gives the group other pictures of insects, or makes them on the blackboard : insects with beautiful coloured wings, insects with numbers of legs, and insects with poison in their tails.

"There are a great number of different sorts of insects. Some of them are very beautiful, and some, like the bee, are able to give wounds with their tails. Then there are the ants who have their house in a little mountain of earth, and the fly, who makes a buzz round our windows.

The insect in the picture comes from very warm countries. He is a great trouble, because his bite gives great pain. He has wings, but they are folded against his body and we are not able to see them in the picture. We see only his six long thin legs, his long thin body, and the little round point which is his head.

Take another look at the picture and say **'insekt.**"

Apparatus ii is now given out. Everyone gets some sticks and one round marker.

" I will make a picture of the insect which you are to make with your sticks. First put the little marker for his head. His body is in two parts, a short part at the top, then a long part under that. He has six legs, but they are all bent, so we will have to have two sticks for

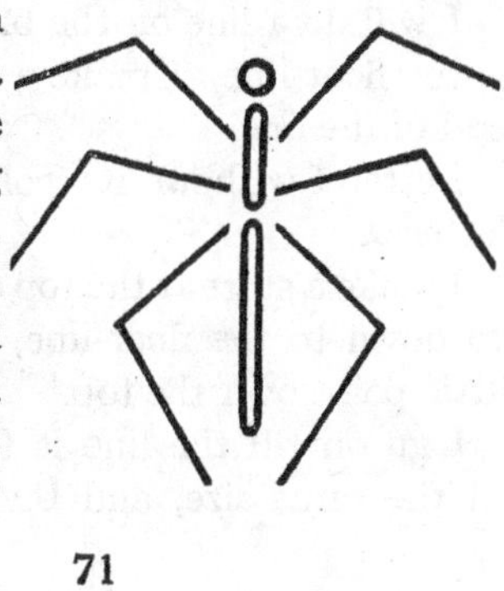

every leg. All the legs are joined on to the top part of the body, three legs on one side and three on the other. Now make your insect of sticks.

All take another look at the wall-card. Is anyone able to say the name of the letter?"

" It is **i**."

" See how we make **i** from your insect of sticks.

Take off his legs, now make his head go high up over his body. Naturally, you would not do this to a living insect, but only to a picture."

The apparatus is now put away and the pencils, white paper, and rulers are given out.

" Make a line on your paper with the ruler and pencil. We are going to make a line of letter **i**'s."

I will do a line on the blackboard. This is the floor-line. I make a start at the left end of the line.

Letter **i** without its point is as tall as letter **ɔ**.

I make a start at the top of the letter and go down to the floor-line, then I put the little point over the top.

I go on till the line is full. My **i**'s are all the same size, and the same distance from one another, and they are all very straight.

Put out your hands and we will make letter **i** in the air.

Down you go, and come to a stop at the floor line ; now put the little point high over the top.

Now make **i** in the air with one hand at a time.

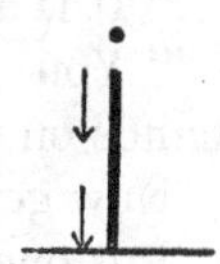

Everyone say **i**-for-insect.

Now make the line of letters on your paper."

The teacher goes round to everyone and sees that the pencil is being used in the right way, the letter made rightly, and the two hands used in turn.

**4**

**l**-for-leg

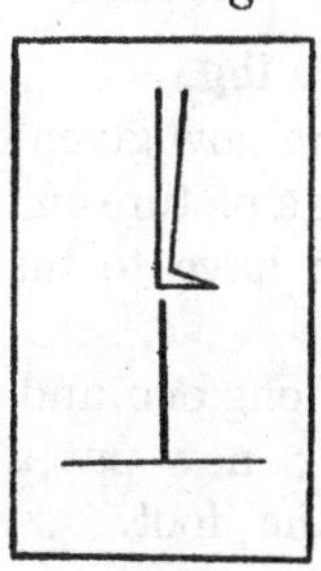

*Apparatus :*

(i) Sticks.

(ii) White paper, rulers, and pencils.

The teacher puts a finger against the wall-card '1.'

" What is this picture?"

" It is a leg."

" You all have two legs. Put your hands on them.

Now get up on your two legs.

Put one leg straight up in the air. Now put it down on the floor like the one in the picture.

It is a long straight line down to the floor, then a short line forward for the foot.

Make the form of two legs in the air with your hands.

Put your hands up high, then down to the floor and a little way forward for the foot.

Everyone say **leg.**

The sticks are now given out.

" I will make a picture on the blackboard of the leg you have to make with your sticks.

Take a very long one, and put it straight up for the leg ; now put a little one on the end for the foot.

Everyone make the leg with sticks.

Now take another look at the wall-card.

Is anyone able to give the name of the letter?"

" It is **l**."

" See how the leg made with sticks is like the letter **l**.

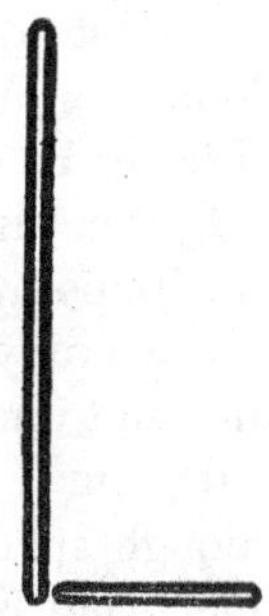

When we make the letter, we do not make the foot—only the leg ; so take off the little stick for the foot, and you have the letter.

Take a look at the wall-card and see if it is not so.

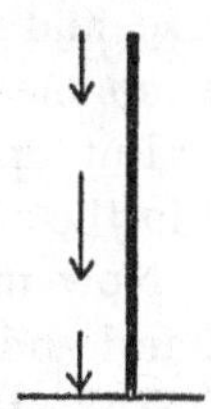

Now you have the letter **l**-for-leg.

Everyone say **l**-for-leg one after another.

Make a line of these letters with the long sticks.

They will all be very tall and straight.

Take care that not one of them is bent and that they are all the same size.

They are a line of letter **l**'s."

The sticks are now taken back.

Everyone is given a pencil and white paper and has the use of a rule.

"First take the rule and make the floor-line. We are going to make a line of letter **l**'s with pencils.

Letter **l** is twice as tall as letter **i** without its point.

Put out your hands—one for the floor-line and one for the top of letter **i**. Now put your top hand up so that there is enough space for another **i** over the first one. That is how high letter **l** is.

I will do a line of **l**'s on the blackboard. This is my floor-line. I make a start at the top of the letter and come straight down. I go on making these letters till the line is full. Every one of them is the same size and they are all the same distance from one another.

Put up your hands, and we will make **l** in the air.

Now make it in the air first with one hand and then with the other.

Take your pencils and make a line of letters on paper.

Keep in mind the line of sticks and do not let the letters be bent or of different sizes."

When everyone is working the teacher goes round giving help.

5

a-for-apple

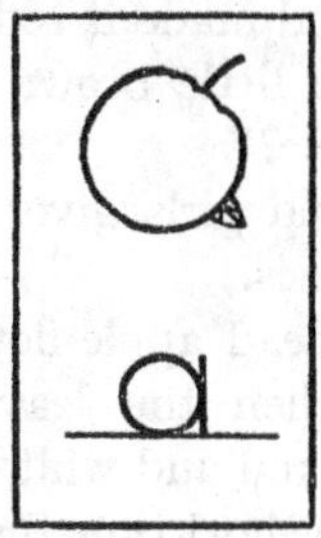

*Apparatus :*

(i) An apple with leaf.

(ii) Coloured chalks and paper.

(iii) Letter-makers.

(iv) Pencils, white paper, and rulers.

(*Note :* This is the first letter of complex form to be taken and it is important to take great care that it is well fixed in the minds of the group).

The teacher takes up the apple and puts it in front of the boys and girls.

" What is this?"

" It is an apple."

" Make your hands round as if you had an apple in them."

Everyone makes a cup of his hands.

" Now give attention to the colour of the apple.

It is green and red. At one time it was all green, but the sun came and gave it a warm touch and made it red on one side.

What is the little brown mark on one end of the apple?"

The boys and girls give their ideas of what the mark is.

" It is the dead apple-flower. Early in the spring, when the leaves are small, the little light red and white apple flowers come out. In a short time they get smaller, and their beautiful colours go, while the baby apple gets greater and greater.

When the apple is full size the little brown mark is all there is to be seen of the beautiful flower."

The teacher, pointing to the apple stem, says:

" What is this?"

The boys and girls make attempts to say what this little stick is. With the help of the teacher they make the discovery that at one time it kept the apple fixed onto the tree, and that through this little stem first the flower and then the fruit got its food.

" The stem is at the opposite end of the apple from the dead flower.

What is this other thing fixed onto the apple stem?"

" It is a green leaf."

" It came away with the apple when the apple was taken from the tree .

I will make a picture of an apple on the blackboard.

The apple was first of all a little light red flower. We take our light red chalk and make a round mark. Now the growth of the young apple is starting. The young apple is green, so I put a green line round the flower. I make the chalk go round and round, and the little apple gets greater and greater till it is its full size. We saw that when the apple had got to its full size the little red flower had gone brown. So we take a brown chalk and go over the light red mark and make it brown. Now the sun comes and sends its warm rays to the top side of the apple, making it red.

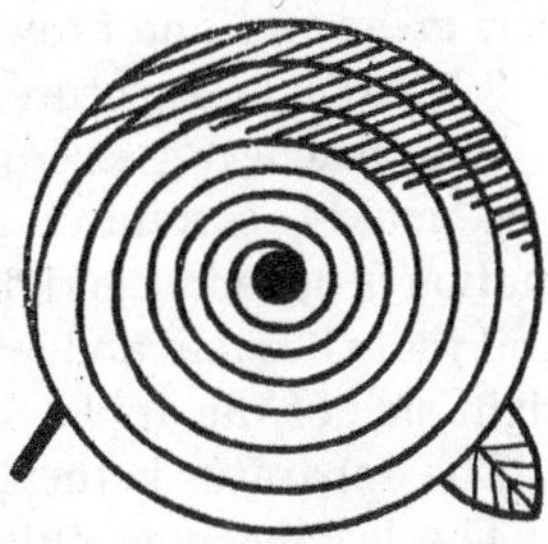

We go over the green on that side with our red chalk. The stem is on the opposite side of the apple so we are not able to see it all, but if we have a good look we will see the small end of it coming from under the apple, and the leaf putting its nose over the top. The stem is brown and the leaf is green.

All say **'apl** with care."

Apparatus is now given out. Everyone gets green, red, and brown chalk and paper.

" Now make a picture of the apple."

The teacher goes round giving help. She makes certain that the screw-like motion is done in the right to left direction, and that the stem and leaf are made on the right side of the apple.

The apparatus is then put away.

The teacher now puts up the wall-card ' a.' She puts a finger on the picture.

" Here is the apple. Is anyone able to give the name of the letter?"

" It is **a**."

Everyone says **a** one after the other.

The letter-makers are now given out.

" We are going to make letter **a** with these black bits.

Put the bit of white paper flat on the table.

See the floor-line. Put your finger on it. Now take the black circle and the stick with two round marks (. .), and make an **a**. Letter **a** is seated on the line."

The teacher goes round and makes certain that everyone has got the form of the letter right, and the apparatus is then put away.

" I will make letter **a** on the blackboard. I make a start as if I were going to do **ɔ** but I do not come to a stop as I did for **ɔ**. I go on up, then down in a straight line to the floor-line. I do not take off the chalk from the start to the end.

Put out your hands and we will make **a** in the air.

Up, round and up, then down in a straight line."

They do this a number of times, sometimes with two hands together, and sometimes with one hand at a time.

" Take a seat on the floor with your knees up to your chin. Now put your head down. You are the apple seated on the floor. Your legs and feet are the stem. **Put one hand out at**

the top of your knees. That is the leaf.

Let us see again how you would make a letter **a**. Make a start at the front of your head, go down your back to the floor and on up to the ends of your fingers, then down the front of your legs to your feet.

Jimmy will make an apple of himself on the table and we will see how we make **a** of him.

Now Pat will do it for Jimmy to see."

Apparatus is now given out—pencils, white paper, and rulers.

" Make a pencil line with the ruler for the floor-line, like the one I did on the blackboard.

Then we will do an **a** seated on the line.

Take care that the top of the straight line is not higher or lower than the top of the round part of the letter. Make one letter for me to see."

The teacher will take special care that this letter is rightly made. It is the first letter in which two parts are joined together, and it is important to be certain that there are no errors in making the join.

At times the boys and girls put down their pencils and make the letter again in the air, to get the right direction well fixed in their minds.

6

t-for-tree

*Apparatus :*

(i) Sticks and markers.
(ii) Phonograph and record.
(iii) White paper, pencils, and rulers.

The teacher puts up the wall-card 't' for everyone to see.

" What is this picture?"

" It is a tree."

" Get up from your seats and put out your arms as if you were a tree.

Your feet are coming out of the earth, your body is the tall, straight, middle part of the tree, and your arms are the branches.

Keep your eyes shut and see in your mind the leaves which are on your branches.

It is summer-time. Let your fingers be

moved as if by a soft wind going through the leaves.

Now it is the fall. Your leaves are no longer green, they are beautiful shades of red and yellow.

Now the cold wind comes.

I will put a record on the machine ; it is the voice of the wind, and you will let your branches go back and forward to the sound of the music.

Now come to a stop. It is a quiet day. There is no wind.

Your eyes are open now. There are no leaves on your branches.

It is winter-time, and you are only a tall straight tree with two branches.

Go to your seats and we will make the tree with sticks and markers."

Apparatus is now given out. Everyone gets brown sticks and green, yellow, and red markers.

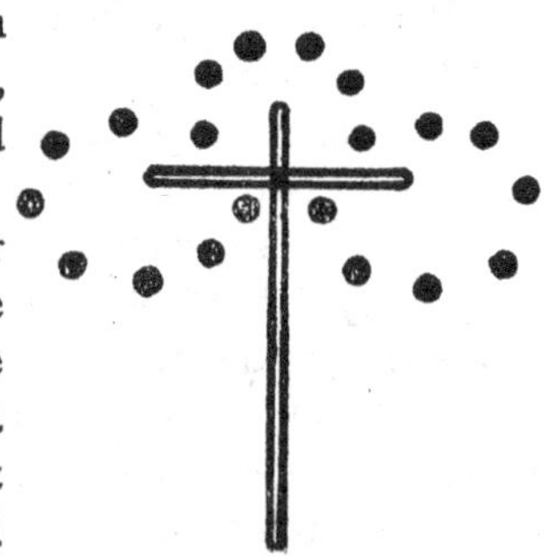

"Take another look at the picture of the tree. It has a long straight brown body and two branches, one on one side and one on the other, a little way from the top. You will have to have a very long brown stick for the body and two very small ones for the branches.

The coloured markers are for the leaves. Put them round the branches and the tree top. Get to work and make the tree."

When they have done this they all say **triː** with care.

" Now have another look at the wall-card.

Is anyone able to give the name of the letter?"

" It is **t**$^{ə}$."

Everyone says **t**$^{ə}$ in turn. The teacher makes certain that they do not say **tr**.

" Now see how we make **t**$^{ə}$ from the tree we made.

Let the fall wind come and send all the leaves falling to the earth. There is only the tall straight tree now, with its body and branches."

The apparatus is now put away.

" Letter **t**$^{ə}$ is made of two straight lines.

I will do one on the blackboard for you to see.

Here is the floor-line.

I put my chalk high up over the line.

Letter **t** is tall, but not as tall as letter **l**.

Down I go in a straight line to the floor. Then I take off the chalk.

Now I put on the branches. Near the top I make a small straight line across the first one.

Everyone say $\mathbf{t}^{ə}$-for-tree.

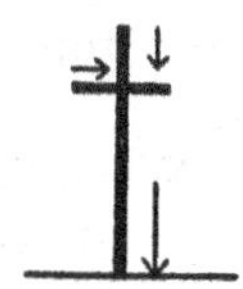

We will make it in the air.

Put out your hands, one for the floor-line and one for the top of the letter **l**.

Now let your top hand come down a little. That is how tall letter $\mathbf{t}^{ə}$ is.

Make a start at the top and go down to the floor-line. Now put in the little branch line."

White paper, pencils, and rulers are now given out.

" Make the floor-line with the ruler, and do a line of letter $\mathbf{t}^{ə}$'s."

The teacher goes round giving help.

7

## WORD-BUILDING

*Apparatus :*

(i) Letter-squares.

(ii) Paper, pencils, and rulers.

(iii) Printed lists of words taken.

" We are going to put our letters together to make words."

Everyone is given a parcel of printed letters. There are two of letters ***o, i, l, a,*** and ***t.***

" Take out the letters and put them face up on the table.

Word-building is not hard. We put two or more letters side by side and say their names quickly.

Take letter **i** and then put letter **t**ᵊ by its side.

Say their names very quickly: **it** and you get ' it.'

' It ' is the word used in place of the name of a thing which has been named or pointed out before.

We say ' *It* is on the table ' in place of ' The ruler is on the table ' when everyone sees that what we are talking about is the ruler.

Now take the letter **a** and put the letter **t**ᵊ after it.

Say them quickly. What is the word?"

" It is **at.**"

" We say ' Jane is *at* school,' or ' Bob is *at* the table.'

Now put letter **t**$^{e}$, then letter **i**, and then two letter **l**'s.

When two letters come together, they make the same sound as if there was only one letter. The two letter **l**'s say **l**.

Take the first two letters of this group and see what they say together.

**t-i, ti.**

Now put on the last letter, **ti-l, til.**

Great care is necessary in teaching word-building. It is best to take the first two letters together first, and then put the other letters on the end, one after another, like this :—

Example ' sent.' **s-e, se ; se-n, sen ; sen-t, sent.**

The group will have to go over the letters a great number of times before they are able to do building with comfort. At first it is best to let them say the letters out loud while they are doing the building, but after a time they keep quiet till they are able to give the complete word.

" The letters on your letter-squares are in print. The letters on the wall-cards are in writing.

The letter **a** in print is different from what it is in writing, but the other letters are almost the same. You saw from your letter-bricks that most of the printed letters have little lines at their feet, and sometimes at their heads.

We put the letters of a word near to one another, and make a space between words wide enough for a letter."

The letter-squares are now taken back, and the printed lists are given out.

" Here are the words in print.

Get pencils, paper, and rulers, and make a floor-line. Now put the printed words into writing."

**8**

**f-for-flower**

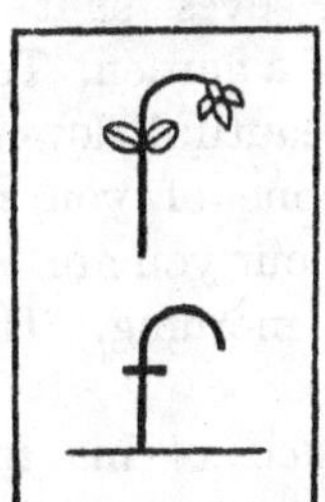

***Apparatus :***

(i) Plasticine.
(ii) Letter-makers.
(iii) Paper, pencils, and rulers.

The teacher puts the wall-card 'f' in front of the group.

" What is this picture?"

" It is a flower."

" It has a long straight stem, bent over at the top, with the flower at the end. There are two little leaves on the stem. Sometimes flowers do not have bent stems but put their heads straight up. We are going to make one with a bent stem like this.

Get on your feet and put your heads down.

Your body is the stem and your head is the flower. Put your hands in position for the two leaves.

Keep your eyes shut and let your thoughts be of a garden. Together you are a group of beautiful flowers in a flower-bed. Every one of you make up your mind what colour you are.

It is early morning. The sun is now getting up.

At the touch of his rays you come awake. Your eyes are now open, and very slowly you put up your head.

Give the sun a smile. It is day.

Now the day is ended, and it is time to go to sleep.

When the sun goes to bed you slowly put down your head and go to sleep.

Now you are again the flower in the picture, sleeping on its bent stem.

Go to your seats.

See how I make the flower with Plasticine. First I make a long thin roll. That is the stem. I put it on the board, making a curve at the top.

Now I make the parts of the flower. First I make three small balls, then I get them flat. These three parts together make the flower.

I get the flower fixed onto the stem, then I make two eggs for the leaves. I get them flat, and put them side by side on the stem.

Now the flower is complete.

Everyone say **'flauə.**"

The Plasticine is now given out and everyone makes a flower. When it is done the Plasticine is taken back.

" Have another look at the wall-card.

**Is anyone able to give the name of the letter?"**

" It is **f**."

" **f** is a very quiet letter. In saying it, we do not make any use of our voice, only of our lips and breath."

Everyone says **f** in turn.

The letter-makers are now given out.

" Take the stick with three marks on it (. . .), a half-circle, and the stick with one mark (.), and make **f**-for-flower."

Everyone says **f**-for-flower.

" Put away the letter-makers and see me do ' **f**-for-flower ' on the blackboard.

**f** is a tall letter with its feet on the floor-line, so we make a start high up. Over we go in a curve to the left, then straight down to the floor.

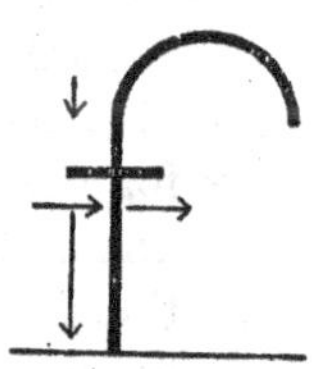

Last we put across it the little stick for the leaves.

Make it in the air, first with two hands together, then with one hand after the other."

Paper, pencils, and rulers are given out.

" Make a floor-line, and then do a line of letter **f**'s on your paper."

The teacher goes round giving help.

## 9

**k$^{e}$-for-curve**

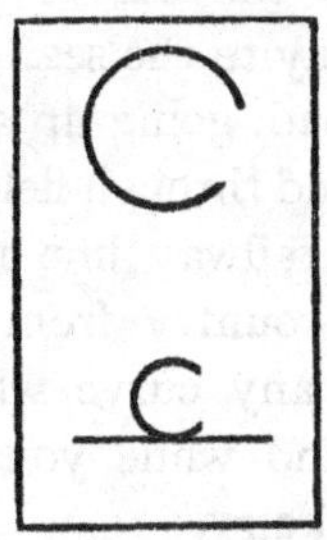

*Apparatus :*

(i) Finger paints.
(ii) Paper, pencils, and rulers.

The teacher makes a straight line with coloured chalk on the blackboard.

"What is that?"

"It is a line."

"It is a *straight* line."

The teacher makes a curved line on the blackboard.

"What is that?"

"It is a curved line."

"A curve is a sort of round line. A line may be curved in a number of different ways."

The teacher makes curves of all forms and in all directions on the blackboard.

" Put out your hands and we will make curves in the air.

First make the curves of a beautiful river on its way to the sea.

Now the road, going up and down over the country and through fields to the town.

Now do a railway line making curves through the country from one town to another. Do any curve which comes to your mind, and while you are doing it, say the word **kəːrv.**

Now we are going to make a special curve."

The teacher makes a curve like a letter ' c ' in the air.

" It goes up, over to the left, down and round, and up again.

See what it is like on the blackboard.

It is like a circle which is not quite joined."

Finger paints are now given out.

" We are going to make curves with the finger paints. Let me see what curves you are able to make."

When they have done, they put the papers up to get dry.

Everyone takes a look at the work of the others to see the different curves.

The paints are put away.

The teacher now takes down the wall-card ' c.'

" See ! There is the special curve we made in the air.

Is anyone able to say the name of the letter?"

" It is **k.**$^{ə}$"

Everyone says **k**$^{ə}$-for-curve.

" **k**$^{ə}$ is seated on the line on the blackboard. See me do it again.

I make a start as if I was going to do letter **ɔ**, but I do not quite make the join."

Paper, pencils, and rulers are given out.

" Make the floor-line.

Now do letter **k**$^{ə}$ in the air again.

Make a start at the right, then go round to the left and back almost to the starting-point.

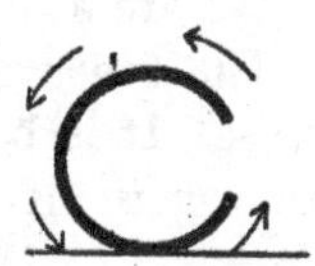

Make a line of the letters on your paper."

The teacher goes round giving help.

*Word-building*

cat

## 10

### e-for-egg-cup

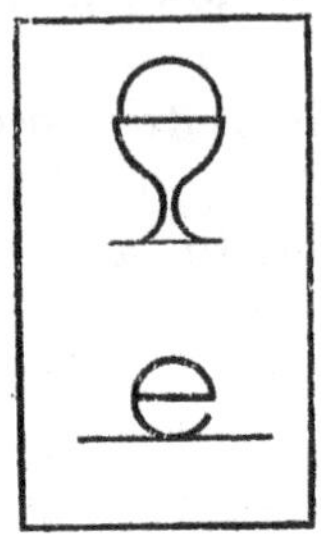

*Apparatus :*

(i) Plasticine.

(ii) Paper, pencils, and rulers.

" Keep your eyes shut and let your thoughts be of the country.

We are at a farm-house.

The fowls outside are making a great noise. It is because one of them has put an egg in her box. We will go and get it.

We will take it into the house and have it cooked.

Put it in an egg-cup, and it is ready for our tea.

See ! Here is the picture."

The teacher puts her finger on the wall-card ' e.'

" Now see me make the egg in the egg-cup in Plasticine

I first make my Plasticine into a round ball. Then I make it like an egg by rolling it so that it gets a little longer.

I put a little flat bit onto one end for the foot of the egg-cup.

Now it is able to keep upright.

See in the picture the line round the middle. That is the top edge of the egg-cup. I make that line with my thumb-nail.

Now we have an egg in an egg-cup.

Everyone say **eg**.

Now make one with your Plasticine."

Plasticine is given out to everyone.

When they have made their egg-cups and everyone has seen the others' work the Plasticine is put away.

" Take another look at the wall-card.

Is anyone able to give the name of the letter?"

" It is **e**."

Everyone says **e**.

" See me make it on the blackboard.

First I do the line we made for the edge of the egg-cup. It is a straight line. I do not take my chalk off, but go on up and over to make the top half of the egg, then down and round almost back to the edge of the egg-cup again.

**That is e.**

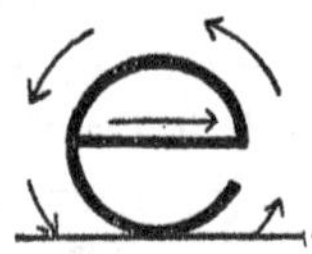

Everyone say **e**-for-egg.

Put out your hands and we will do it in the air."

They do this motion in the air a great number of times, with two hands together, and with one hand after the other.

It is a hard letter, and it is necessary to do it over and over before the direction is clearly fixed in their minds.

White paper and pencils are given out.

"First we will do letter **e** without the floor-line. Take your pencils and make letter **e**'s all over the paper, great ones and small ones."

The rulers are now given out.

"Now, on the clean side of your paper, make a floor-line.

See me do **e** on the floor-line. I make the straight line a little distance from the floor-line, then over I go down to the floor-line and up again, giving it a touch on my way round.

Letter **e** is the same size as letter **ɔ**.

Make a line of letter **e**'s.

The teacher goes round giving help.

*Word-building*

let left lets

11

**r-for-rail**

*Apparatus :*

(i) Plasticine.
(ii) Paper, pencils, rulers.
(iii) Letter-makers.

The teacher takes the wall-card ' r ' and puts it face down on the table.

" There was a man who had a great desire for a garden. He put some seeds into the earth in the hope that after a time plants would come up and get tall and have beautiful flowers.

After a week or two the plants did come up.

They put their little green noses through the brown earth, and the man was very pleased.

Then a sad thing took place. One morning, when the man was looking from his window, he saw something which made his heart go down into his boots. The little green plants had all been crushed down to the earth.

The cats and dogs which go about at night had been all over the garden. They had gone running here and there in the dark without seeing where they were going, and so the young plants were all crushed.

The man was very sad, but after a short time he said to himself ' Possibly, if I put in some more plants, the animals will not go on them.'

He did so, and these little plants put up their heads as the others had done, and the man was very pleased.

One day he went for a walk. When he was coming back, the sound of young voices came to his ears.

Boys and girls were playing round his house. They were so interested in their play that they did not see where they were going, and they had been running over the flower-beds, so that the young plants were crushed again.

' Oh!' said the man. ' You are bad boys

and girls; see what you have done to these little plants!'

When they saw what they had done, the boys and girls were very unhappy, and went away hanging their heads.

The poor man then said 'It was my greatest desire to have a garden, but I will never be able to have one, because every time the plants get a start somebody goes walking over them.'

He said this to one of his friends.

'Why don't you put rails round your garden?' said the friend.

'What a good idea!' said the man. 'Why didn't I do that before?'

He went off to the store to get the rails, and the storekeeper let him see the different sorts he kept. There were rails made of wood and rails made of iron, there were high rails and low rails, and rails of all colours.

After much thought the man took a line of tall, strong, iron rails and went to his garden to get it fixed.

The rails were tall iron rods, with a space of ten or twelve inches between them, and joined near the top by half-circles of iron. The rods had sharp points at the top so that no one would be able to get over them into the garden.

With a smile on his face the man again put in his plants, and in a very short time he had a garden full of the most beautiful flowers.

Now he is seated in the shade of his trees, a very happy man."

The wall-card 'r' is now turned over.

"Take a look at this card.

This is like the rails the man put round his garden."

The Plasticine is now given out.

" We are going to make a line of rails. See how I make it.

We make a long roll of Plasticine and get it cut into rods of the same size.

Then we make points at the top of them all, and put them in a line.

Now we make another roll and get it cut into shorter bits. We make these bits into half-circles and get them fixed between the rods.

Everyone say **reil.**

Now make the rails with your Plasticine.

Take a look at the wall-card.

Is anyone able to give the name of the letter?"

" It is **r**." Everyone say **r**.

" See how like the rails it is.

Take away all the rails but one. The one rod with its half-circle is almost the same as the letter on the card.

Put the Plasticine in its drawer.

See me make **r** on the blackboard.

I make a start at the top and go down as for letter **i**, but then I go up the same line again, almost to the top, and over to the right to make the half-circle.

I do not take off the chalk till the letter is done.

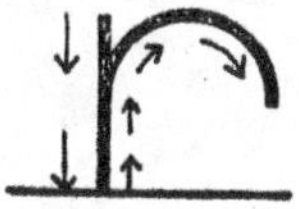

Put out your hands and do it in the air."

The letter-makers are now given out.

" Take the stick with two marks (. .), and the half-circle, and make **r**."

It has its feet on the floor-line.

Now get onto your feet and put one arm out to the side. Get the arm bent into a half-circle.

You are letter **r**-for-rail.

Say **r**-for-rail.

To make you, I make a start at your

head, go down to your feet, come up again to your neck, then over your arm to your fingers.

Put out your hands and do it in the air."

They do this a great number of times in the air. It is a hard letter, and the teacher has to make certain that the muscles get quite used to the right motions.

White paper, pencils, and rulers are given out.

" Make a line of letter **r**'s. They are as tall as letter **i** without the point on it, and they have all to be upright and of the same size."

The teacher goes round giving help.

12

**n**-for-nose

*Apparatus:*

(i) Letter-makers.

(ii) White paper, pencils, and rulers.

The teacher takes down the wall-card 'n' and puts her finger on the picture.

"What is this picture?"

"It is a man's nose."

"You all have a nose. Put your finger on it.

The one in the picture is a great bent nose.

Put your first finger out and make it bent over like the nose in the picture.

Everyone say **nouz.**

Go to your blackboards and with your chalks make a picture of a man with a great nose.

Now take a look at the letter on the wall-card.

Is anyone able to say what it is?"

"It is **n.**"

"Everyone say **n.**"

The letter-makers are given out.

"Letter **n** is very like letter **r** but it has one more stick with its foot on the floor-line.

Take the stick with two marks (. .), the half-circle, and the stick with one mark (.), and make letter **n.**

Everyone say '**n**-for-nose.'

Put back the letter-makers.

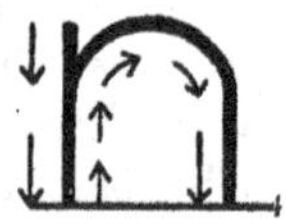

See me make **n** on the blackboard.

I do letter **r** and then go on down to the floor.

Put out your hands and do it in the air. Down, up the same line again almost to the top, then over to the right in a half-circle, then on down to the floor-line. We do not take off the pencil till the letter is done."

Paper, pencils, and rulers are given out.

" Make the floor-line.

Letter **n** is as tall as letter **r**.

Make a line of letters ' **n**-for-nose '."

The teacher goes round giving help.

*Word-building*

not ten

## 13

**m**-for-mountain

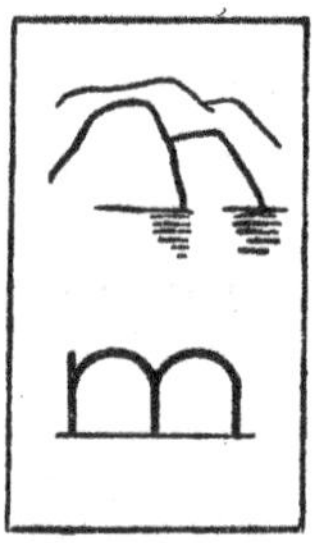

*Apparatus :*

(i) Pictures of mountains.
(ii) Plasticine.
(iii) Letter-makers.
(iv) White paper, pencils, and rulers.

" Today we are going to give our attention to mountains. Some of you may have seen a mountain. If not, it will not be hard for you to get an idea of one.

Mountains are great tall masses of earth and stone, frequently thousands of feet high. Sometimes their tops are sharp and pointed, and sometimes they are round.

Keep your eyes shut and say to yourself that you are in a mountain country.

You are in a green field and in the distance are two mountains. They are round at the top and not very high, with fields and trees all over them. At the back of these two mountains is a line of very high mountains. They have no trees or grass on them, and they are made not of soft earth but of hard stone. They go up and up, straight up into the sky, and their pointed tops are covered with snow.

See their white, sharp-pointed tops in the sky.

Now come back to the smaller mountains

in front. We are going to make a journey over them.

Put out your hands ; they will make the journey for you.

Now they are at the foot of the first mountain.

Make them go up and over it, down into the lowland between the two mountains, then up the side of the second mountain, over and down again."

The pictures of mountains are then given out. Have as great a number of different views as possible.

There is a general discussion about the pictures.

The Plasticine is then given out.

" The Plasticine board is the flat earth, and we are going to make mountains on it of Plasticine.

Get to work and make your flat board into mountain country. The mountains are of different sizes, some round and some pointed."

They may do this work in small groups, three or four of them making mountains at the same board.

" Everyone say **'mauntin.**"

Put away the Plasticine."

The teacher puts up the wall-card ' m ' in front of the group.

" What is this picture?"

" It is a picture of mountains."

" It is the two round mountains we went over in our journey.

See the letter. Is anyone able to give its name?"

" It is **m**."

" **m** is a strange noise. We keep our lips shut when we say it.

Everyone say **m** in turn.

See how much the letter is like the picture. There are the two round tops, and there is the lowland between.

The letter has one thing more. It has a straight line at the front before we come to the mountains."

The letter-makers are given out.

" Letter **m** is like letter **n** but it has one more half-ircle and one more straight line. It is as high as letter **n** but it is wider. Its feet are on the line.

Take one stick with two marks (. .), two sticks with one mark (.), and two half-circles, and make the letter.

That is **m**-for-mountain.

Everyone say it in turn.

Put back the letter-makers.

See me make **m** on the blackboard.

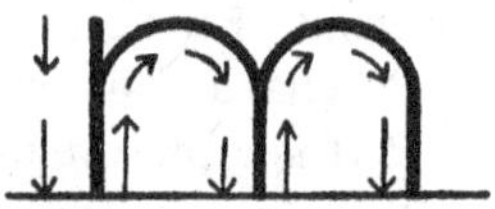

It has all its three feet on the line.

I make a start with a straight line down, as for letter **n.** Without taking the chalk off, I go back over it almost up to the top; then over I go to the right to make the first mountain, down to the floor, up the same line again, over and down to the floor again.

Put out your hands, and we will do it in the air."

They do it in the air till the teacher is certain that they have got the direction firmly fixed in their minds. Then the white paper, pencils, and rulers are given out.

" First make the floor-line, then do a line of letter **m**'s."

The teacher goes round giving help.

*Word-building*

man am from

14

**b$^{e}$-for-brush**

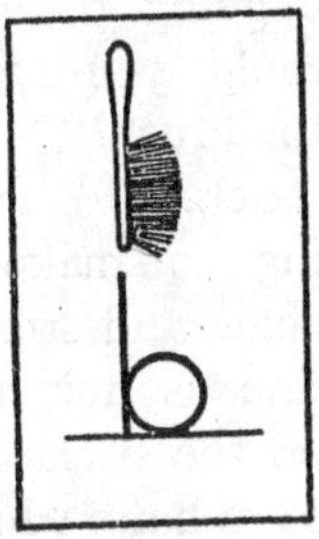

*Apparatus* :

(i) Plasticine and sticks.
(ii) Letter-makers.
(iii) Paper, pencils, and rulers.

The teacher takes down the wall-card ' b ' and puts it up in front of the group.

" What is that picture?"

" It is a brush."

" It is a long bit of wood with a brush-part of stiff hairs fixed at one end.

Someone come and put a finger on the hairs.

That is the part which gets things brushed.

Now someone put a finger on the other end.

That is the part we take in our hands when we do the brushing.

The hairs are fixed into the wood back in little groups to make the brush.

If you were going to make a brush, which part would you make first, the wood back or the brush?"

"The wood back."

"I am going to make a brush of Plasticine and sticks.

The Plasticine is for the wood part, and the sticks for the little groups of hairs which make the brush.

I take a bit of Plasticine and make it into a thick roll.

I make the middle of the roll a little thinner, then I make one end, the end which is going to be the brush-part, flat.

I put in the sticks to make the little groups of hairs.

That is a brush.

Everyone say **brʌʃ**."

The Plasticine and sticks are now given out.

When all the boys and girls have made a brush, the apparatus is taken back and the letter-makers given out.

" Take another look at the wall-card.

Is anyone able to give the name of the letter?"

" It is **b**$^{ə}$."

Everyone says it.

" Now make **b**$^{ə}$ with the letter-makers.

The tall straight part of the letter is the wood, and the short round part at the side is the brush.

Take the stick with four marks (. . . .) and a circle. Take care to get the round brush part fixed well onto the wood part. The letter is seated on the line.

Put away the apparatus.

See how I do **b**$^{ə}$ on the blackboard.

I make the long wood part first, and I do all the letter without lifting my chalk.

I put the chalk at the top as we did for letter **l**, and down I go to the floor-line. Then up a little way, then over to the right in a most beautiful circle, coming round and meeting the straight line again, so that it is not possible for anyone to see the join.

That is **b**$^{ə}$ for-brush.

Everyone say it." (The teacher will take care that they do not say **br**).

" Put out your hands and do it in the air."

They do this a great number of times till the teacher is certain they have got the direction well into their heads.

The paper, pencils, and rules are then given out.

" The tall part of letter **b**$^{ə}$ is as tall as letter **l**, and the round part is the same size as letter **ɔ**. Another **ɔ** put on top of the lower one would have its top level with the top of the tall line.

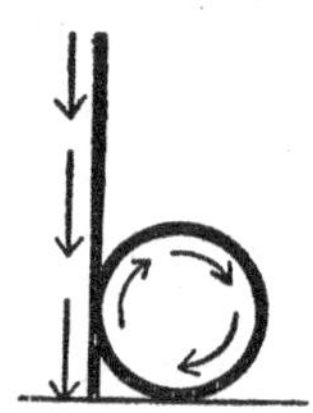

Do a line of letter **b**$^{ə}$'s.

The teacher goes round to give help and to be certain that they are making the letter in the right direction.

*Word-building*

bit bag bell bent

15

**h°-for-house**

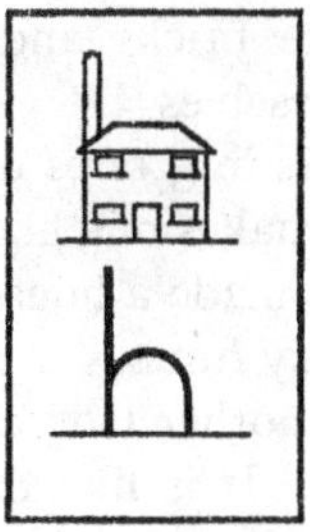

*Apparatus :*

(i) Bricks.
(ii) Letter-makers.
(iii) Paper, pencils, and rulers.

The teacher puts the wall-card 'h' up in front of the group.

"What is this picture?"

"It is a house."

"It is the house of a strange little woodman, and when he made it he made the tall bit at the side first.

What is the use of that tall bit?"

"It is for taking the smoke up from the fire into the air."

"If the smoke did not have a hole to get out by, in a short time the house would be full of it.

Someone put his finger on the tall part where the smoke comes out.

After building the tall part, the woodman put his little house onto the side.

Get out the bricks and make a little house for yourselves."

They do this in groups of three or four. Every group makes one house.

" You have made a house.

Everyone say **haus.**

Now take another look at the wall-card See the letter. It is like the tall bit with the little house at the side.

Is anyone able to say the letter?"

" It is **h**$^{ə}$."

" It is a quiet letter. We do not make use of our voices when we say it, only of our breath.

Everyone say **h**$^{ə}$ with care.

Put back the bricks and get out the letter-makers.

Letter **h**$^{ə}$ has two feet on the floor-line.

The tall part is as tall as letter **l**, and the small part is the same size as letter **n**.

Take the stick with four marks (. . . .), a half-circle, and a stick with one mark (.), and make **h**$^{ə}$.

Everyone say **h**$^{ə}$-for-house.

Put back the letter-makers.

See me do letter **h**$^{ə}$ on the blackboard.

I make a start at the top of the tall part, then go down to the floor-line as I did for letter **l**, but when I get there I do not take off the chalk. I go up the tall line again, almost half way, then over to the right in a half circle and down to the floor-line again.

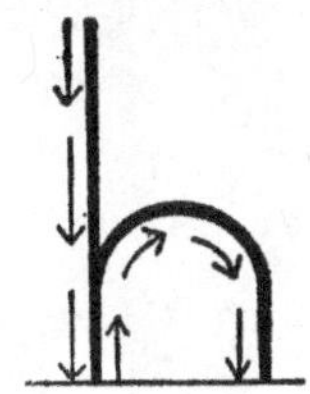

The tall part is twice as high as the small part at the side.

Put out your hands and we will do it in the air."

They do it in the air till the teacher is certain that they have the direction fixed in their minds.

Paper, pencils, and rulers are then given out.

"Make a floor-line and do a line of letter **h**$^{ə}$'s."

See that all the smoke-pipes are as high as one another and that all the houses are the same size."

The teacher goes round giving help.

*Word-building*

hat

## 16

**k**[ə]-for-kick

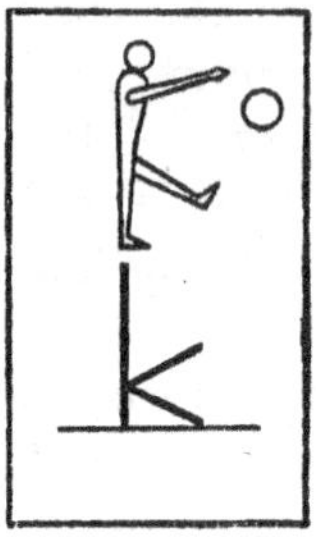

*Apparatus :*

(i) Sticks and Markers.
(ii) Pencils, white paper, and rulers.
(iii) Letter-makers.

The teacher puts the wall-card 'k' on view.

" What is that picture?"

" It is a boy."

" What is he doing?"

" He is giving a kick."

" He is a kicking boy.

Get up and we will all be kicking boys.

Get balanced on one leg and give a high kick with the other.

Now do the same with the other leg.

Now keep one leg very stiff and put the

other up in the air in a kicking position and keep it there.

The boy in the picture has his arm up, so put up one of your arms.

Everyone say **kik**.

Go back to your seats and we will make the kicking boy of sticks and markers."

The sticks and markers are now given out.

" I will do a picture on the blackboard and you will see how to make the kicking boy."

The teacher makes the picture in coloured chalk and gives directions while doing it.

" Put a marker for his head, then a stick under it for his body; under that, another stick for his stiff leg. Now put on his kicking leg, and then his arm.

The other arm is on the other side of his body, out of view.

Get to work and make the kicking boy."

The teacher goes round helping, and taking care that the kicking leg is fixed on at an angle of less than 90°.

" Now take another look at the wall-card.

Is anyone able to give the name of the letter?"

" It is **k**$^{ə}$."

" It has the same sound as **k**$^{ə}$-for-curve. It is a different sign for the same sound.

Everyone say **k**$^{ə}$-for-curve.

Now put out your hands and make **k**$^{ə}$-for-curve in the air.

Now everyone say **k**$^{ə}$-for-kick.

See how your kicking boy may be turned into the letter.

Take off his head and his arm.

Now put his arm where the legs are joined to the body.

That is the letter **k**$^{ə}$-for-kick.

See how I make it on the blackboard.

It is made in a strange way, so give me all your attention.

It is as tall as letter **l**, and I make a start at the very top. I go straight down to the floor-line, and then I do a new thing; I take off the chalk.

Now I make another start about half way up the straight line, a little to the right of it.

From there I go down in a slope till I am touching the tall line, make a turn, and go out again in the direction of the kicking leg to the floor-line. This time the toe is resting on the floor."

The letter-makers are now given out.

" Letter **k**ᵊ has its two feet on the floor-line.

Take the stick with four marks (. . . .) and two sticks with two marks (. .), and make **k**ᵊ.

Say again **k**ᵊ-for-kick.

Put back the letter-makers.

Now put out your hands and we will do the letter in the air."

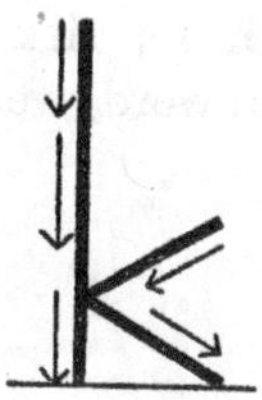

They do it in the air till the teacher is certain that they have the form and the positions of the two starting-points fixed in their minds.

Paper, pencils, and rulers are then given out.

" Make a floor-line, and do a line of letter **k**ᵊ's."

**k**ᵊ has its back to the start of the line and its kicking toe pointing to the end of the line. Make all the letters as tall as one another and very straight."

The teacher goes round giving help.

It is a hard letter and with some of the

less bright boys it will be a help to put points for the positions.

Let them make the tall line, then put a point where the hand comes, then one where the arm and leg are joined to the body, then one for the toe, and last make the lines joining the three in this order.

*Word-building*

black crack kick milk trick
brick clock lock neck

"When we have **k**$^{ə}$-for-curve and **k**$^{ə}$-for-kick coming one after the other in a word, we say only one of them."

17

**d**$^{ə}$-for-danger

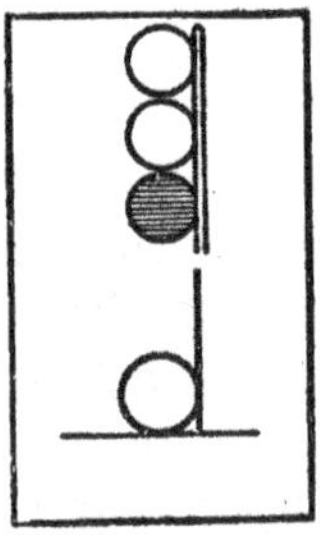

*Apparatus :*

(i) Coloured chalks and blackboards.
(ii) Paper, pencils, and rulers.
(iii) Letter-makers.

" A man was driving his automobile through a town, when he came to a road going across the one he was on.

There were a great number of automobiles coming from the right and the left, and he was not certain when to go across. He took a look up and saw something which gave him help.

There was a tall stick and at the top were three lights, one under the other. The glass over the lowest one was red, over the middle, yellow, and over the top one, green.

Is anyone able to say what those three lights were for ?"

With the help of the teacher, the group makes the discovery that the red light says " Danger," the yellow light says " Take care," and the green light says " Go," and that the three lights take turns at coming on and giving their signs.

The teacher makes a picture of the lights.

" Get up and put out your hands as if they were on the driving-wheel of an automobile.

Go driving round, making the noise of an automobile-horn.

Now take a look at the lights.

I am not able to make them come on in turn, but I will give them a touch one after the other with the rule. When I put the rule on the green light you may go on, because then it will be safe. When I put it on the yellow light, you are to go slowly. And when I put it on the red light, you are to come to a stop, because that says there is danger. When you get ready to go again, make a noise with your horn to let those in the way see that you are coming."

They do this play for some minutes.

" Now go to the blackboards.

Take your coloured chalks and make the three lights on the tall stick."

The teacher then puts the wall-card 'd' for them to see.

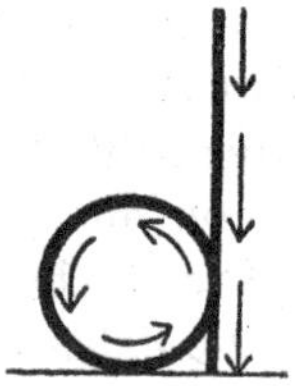

" What is that picture?"

" It is the danger light."

" Is anyone able to give the name of the letter?"

" It is **d**$^{ə}$."

" Everyone say **d**$^{ə}$."

Now get the two top lights on your picture cleaned off with your duster and make the stick as short as the one you see on the wall-card.

See how like the letter your picture is now."

The letter-makers are now given out.

" Letter **d**$^{ə}$ is as tall as letter **l** and it is seated on the floor-line.

Take the circle and the stick with four marks (. . . .) and make **d**$^{ə}$.

The circle is on the left side of the line.

Put away the apparatus.

Now see how I make the letter on the blackboard.

As you see, it is very like letter **b**-for-brush, but it is turned round.

It is not hard not to get them mixed up if you keep this in mind.

When we made the brush it was necessary for us to make the wood part first. So when we made the letter we did the tall part first and put the round part on after.

When the man made the automobile signs he made the lights first, and then got them fixed on the stick.

So I do the round part for the light first. I go round as if for letter **ɔ** but I do not come to a stop when that is done. I go on up to make the stick, then down I come over the same line to the floor-line.

Put out your hands and we will do it in the air."

Paper, pencils, and rulers are given out, and they do a line of **d**'s.

*Word-building*

" Go to the blackboard and make a floor-line.

Now make a letter **b°**. Now a letter **e**. Now a letter **d°**.

What is the word?"

" It is ' bed '."

" Let the two tall ends of the letters be the ends of the bed, and the round parts between, the bed itself. Put a cover on the bed and make it coloured, so that we are not able to see the letters. Put two little balls on top of the

ends of the bed, and then make a cushion at one end.

That is a bed.

If at any time you are uncertain about the way letters **b**$^{ə}$ and **d**$^{ə}$ go, keep in mind the bed. If you do not put them facing in the right direction they will not make the bed."

**18**

**dʒ**-for-jump

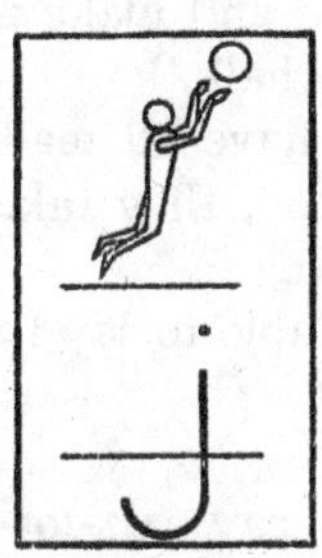

*Apparatus :*

(i) Chalks and blackboards.
(ii) Paper, pencils, etc.
(iii) Letter-makers.

" See this wall-card. What is the picture?"

" It is a boy."

" What is he doing?"

" He is jumping for his ball."

" See, he is in the air, off the floor. His hands are up to get the ball when it comes down.

Get up and put up your hands to get the ball when it comes down.

Now make a jump.

Your feet and legs are bent round and your hands are up for the ball.

You are in the same position as the jumping boy in the picture.

Make one or two more jumps, then go to the blackboard and make a jumping boy with coloured chalk."

When they have all made attempts at the jumping boy, they take another look at the wall-card.

" Is anyone able to say the name of the letter?"

" It is **dʒ**."

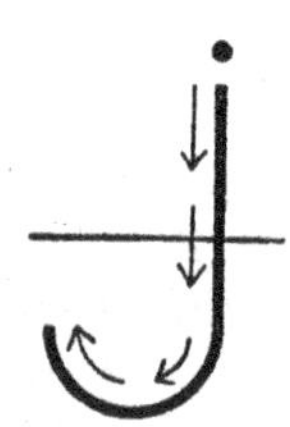

" Everyone say **dʒ**-for-jump.

Take out the letter-makers and go to your seats.

Letter **dʒ** is a very strange letter. The greater part of it is under the floor-line, only a bit, the same size as letter **i**, is on top of the line.

Take the stick with four marks(. . . .), and a half-circle, and a round marker, and make letter **dʒ**.

Put the apparatus back in its place.

See me do letter **dʒ** on the blackboard.

I seem at the start to be making **i**, but I go down in a straight line under the floor-line, then round in a half-circle to the left. Then I put the point high over the top.

Put out your hands and we will do it in the air."

Paper, pencils, and rulers are then given out and they do a line of **dʒ**'s.

The teacher goes round giving help.

19

**g**-for-glasses

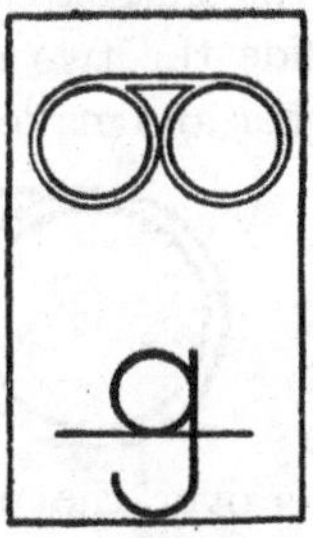

*Apparatus :*

(i) Plasticine or
Cardboard circles, 1 inch and $1\frac{1}{2}$ inches across. Pencils, coloured paper, scissors.

(ii) White paper, pencils, and rulers.

(iii) Letter-makers.

" I am going to make glasses, the sort of glasses you put on your nose to see through if your eyes are not good.

I am going to make them in two ways, and when I have done you may make glasses.

First I make them of coloured paper.

I take the greater of the two cardboard circles and make a pencil line round it.

Then I put the same cardboard circle against the pencil outline and make another circle in pencil, touching the first.

Now I take the smaller cardboard circle and put it inside the two outline circles, one after the other, and make a line round it.

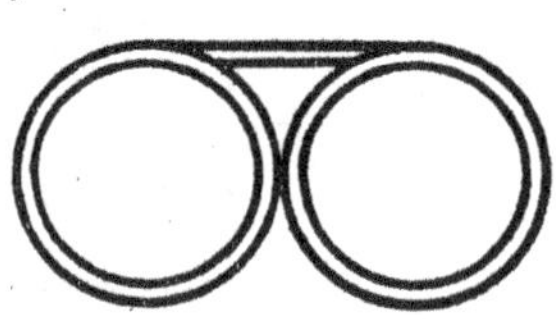

Last I make two little lines joining the top of the two circles for the part which goes over the nose.

Now I take the scissors and get the glasses cut out.

These are glasses of paper.

Now I will make glasses of Plasticine.

I make a long, long roll.

Then I take a little bit off one end, and get the rest cut into two equal parts.

I make these two parts into circles and get them flat.

Then I make a join with the little bit I took off first. I make that bit flat, and the glasses are done.

Everyone say **'glaːsiz.**

I will put my glasses where you are not able to see them and let you make some for yourselves. You may make paper glasses or Plasticine glasses.

Get out the apparatus for whichever sort you are going to make."

When everyone has made his glasses, the teacher takes down the wall-card ' g.'

" Take a look at this picture.

It is a picture of glasses.

Now see the letter.

Is anyone able to give the name of the letter?"

" It is **g**$^{\text{ə}}$."

" Everyone say **g**$^{\text{ə}}$-for-glasses.

Put your glasses on the table in the same

position as the letter in the picture, that is, with one circle over the other and the join at the right side."

The teacher takes out her paper and Plasticine glasses again.

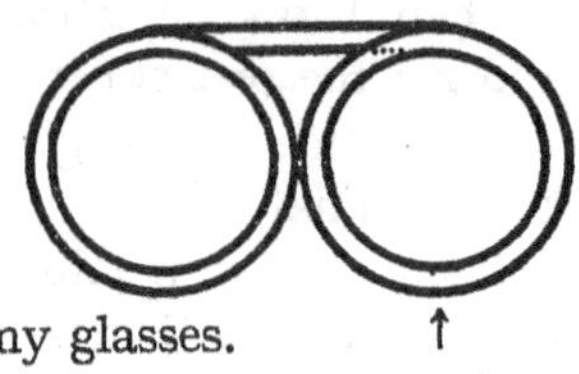

She takes up the paper glasses and the scissors.

" See how I make **g**$^{a}$ out of my glasses.

I make a cut in one circle through to the inner edge of the little join.

Then I make another cut in the middle of the lower half of the same circle, and I have **g**$^{a}$.

I may do the same with the Plasticine glasses.

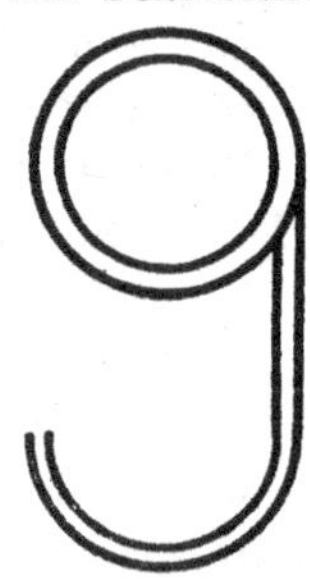

Make **g**$^{a}$ from your glasses.

Put back the apparatus.

Give out the letter-makers.

Letter **g**$^{a}$-for-glasses is seated on the floor-line with its tail going under.

Take the complete circle, one half-circle, and the stick with three marks (. . .), and make **g**$^{a}$.

Put back the apparatus.

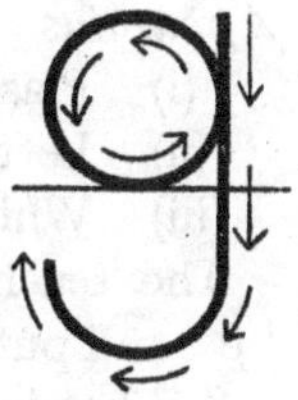

Now see me make $\mathbf{g}^{\circ}$ on the blackboard.

Here is the floor-line.

I make a start in the same way as for letter **a**, but when I have made letter **a** I do not come to a stop. I go on straight down under the line, curving back to the left in a beautiful tail.

Make it in the air.

All get white paper, pencils, and rulers.

Make a floor-line.

Do a line of letter $\mathbf{g}^{\circ}$'s.

The teacher goes round giving help.

*Word-building*

**bag egg glass dog flag leg**

20

$\mathbf{p}^{\circ}$-for-pipe

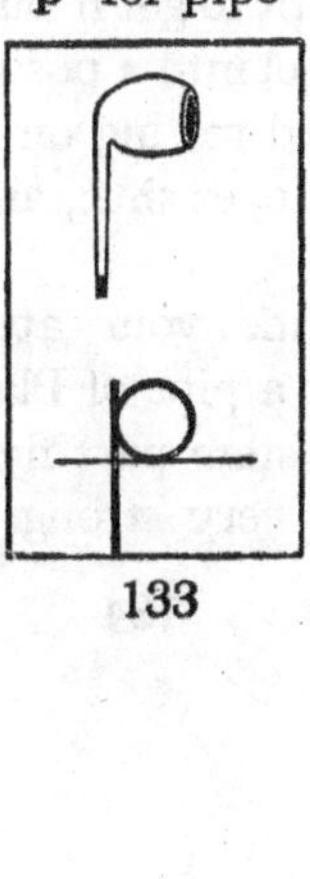

*Apparatus :*

(i) Plasticine.

(ii) Letter-makers.

(iii) White paper, pencils, and rulers.

The teacher takes down the wall-card ' p ' and puts it on view.

" What is this picture?"

" It is a pipe."

" You have all seen a man with a pipe. He puts tobacco into the round end, puts a match to it, and keeps blowing little breaths down the stem, till a slow fire is made which gives out smoke.

Do as you would if you were a man lighting a pipe.

First put in the tobacco.

Now put the pipe in your mouth.

Get the match lighted by giving it a rub on the match box.

Put the match to the tobacco, and take in a deep breath to get it burning.

After that, get into a position of comfort, with your head resting on the back of the seat and your eyes shut, and have a quiet smoke.

Now give me your attention. I am going to make a pipe of Plasticine.

I make the stem part first. It is a roll, not long, but very strong. Then I get a bit for the tobacco end. First I make it into a round ball, and then I put my thumb down hard into the middle to make the hole for the tobacco.

Now I get the stem fixed onto the round end, and there is the pipe.

Everyone say **p**$^{ə}$."

The Plasticine is now given out.

"All make a pipe, as I did, but when it is done do not put it in your mouth. It is not good to put Plasticine in your mouth."

The Plasticine is put away.

"Now take another look at the wall-card.

Is anyone able to say the name of the letter?"

"It is **p**$^{ə}$."

"**p**$^{ə}$ is a very quiet letter. We do not make use of our voices for it, only of our lips and breath. It is the same sound as we make when we send little breaths into the pipe to get the tobacco burning.

See me make the letter **p**$^{ə}$ on the blackboard.

I make the stem first, as I did with the Plasticine. Half the stem goes under the floor-line.

The round part is seated on the floor-line.

Give out the letter-makers.

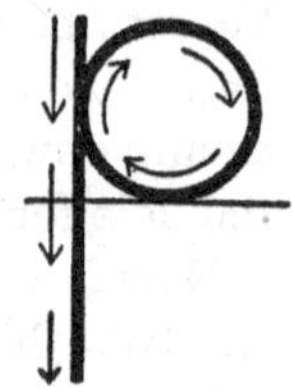

Take the circle and the stick with four marks (. . . .), and make **p**°-for-pipe.

Now put away the letter-makers.

Put out your hands and we will do **p**° in the air.

Starting at the top of the stem, go down, down, then up again on the same line almost to the top, and over to the right to make the round."

They do this till the teacher is certain that they have the direction fixed in their minds.

" Give out the white paper, pencils, and rulers, and all make a floor-line.

See me do one more **p**° on the black-board.

Now do a line of **p**°'s.

Take care to make the stem first and see that all the tails are as long as one another."

The teacher goes round to everyone in turn giving help.

*Word-building*

kept grip help plant print top
drop lip pen pig pin pot

21

ʌ-for-umbrella

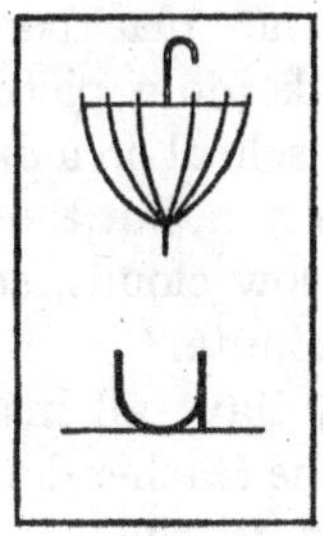

*Apparatus :*

(i) Coloured chalks and blackboards.
(ii) Letter-makers.
(iii) White paper, pencils, and rulers.

The teacher takes down the wall-card ' u ' and puts it before the group.

" What is that picture?"

" It is an umbrella."

" We put an umbrella up on a wet day to keep the rain off. It keeps us dry. That is what umbrellas are for.

I am going to make a picture of boys and girls going to school on a wet day,

Are these umbrellas like the one on the wall-card?"

" No. These umbrellas are up. The one on the wall-card is down."

" Go to the blackboards and with coloured chalks do a picture of boys and girls going to school on a *dry* day.

There is no rain, but the sky is dark and full of great low clouds, so there may be rain at any minute."

When they have all made attempts at the pictures the teacher does one like this.

" See, that is the way the boys and girls have their umbrellas when there is no rain. They are down, like the one on the wall-card.

Make some more pictures of umbrellas, some up and some down.

Take another look at the wall-card.

Is anyone able to give the name of the letter?"

" It is ʌ."

" Everyone say ʌ for-**ʌm'brelə** in turn.

Now see me make letter ʌ on the black-board.

It is not quite like the umbrella. The stick which goes up through the middle of the umbrella is on the right-hand side of the letter. **ʌ** is seated on the line and is the same size as letter **n**.

Give out the letter-makers.

Take the half-circle, the stick with one mark (.), and the stick with two marks (. .), and make letter **ʌ**

Then get your paper turned round so that the letter is upside-down.

Now you have letter **n**.

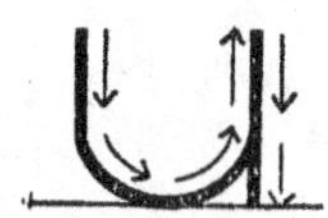

Letter **ʌ** is letter **n** upside-down.

Get the letter turned back to **ʌ** again.

Put away the letter-makers.

See me do the letter on the blackboard again.

I make a start at the top left-hand side and go down and round, and up again, touching the floor-line on the way. Up I go till I am as high as the starting-point, then down over the same line to the floor again.

Put out your hands and make letter **ʌ** in the air."

They do this till they have the direction fixed in their minds.

Pencils, white paper, and rulers are then given out.

" Now make a line of letter ʌ's."

The teacher goes round giving help.

*Word-building*

but rub run bulb cup
gun nut pump cut

22

v-for-vessel

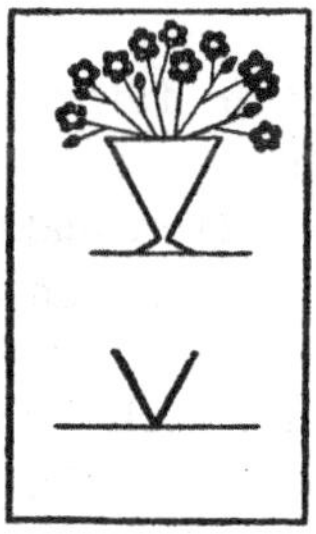

*Apparatus :*

(i) Sticks and coloured markers.

(ii) White paper, pencils, and rulers.

The teacher has put the wall-card ' v ' face down on the table.

" Today we are going to have a new word.

It is ' vessel.'

A vessel may be a number of things.

It may be a ship, or it may be a pot of almost any form for cooking or keeping water in.

Take a look at the one in the picture.

This vessel is wide at the top and gets narrower and narrower till it comes to a point at the base. Its special use is for flowers."

The sticks and coloured markers are now given out.

" See me make the flower-vessel with sticks and markers.

I take three long sticks for the body of the vessel, then a little one for the foot.

Then I put the flowers in it.

I will put sticks for the stems and coloured markers for the flowers.

That is a vessel of flowers.

Everyone say v in turn.

Make a vessel of flowers with your sticks and markers.

Is anyone able to give the name of the letter?"

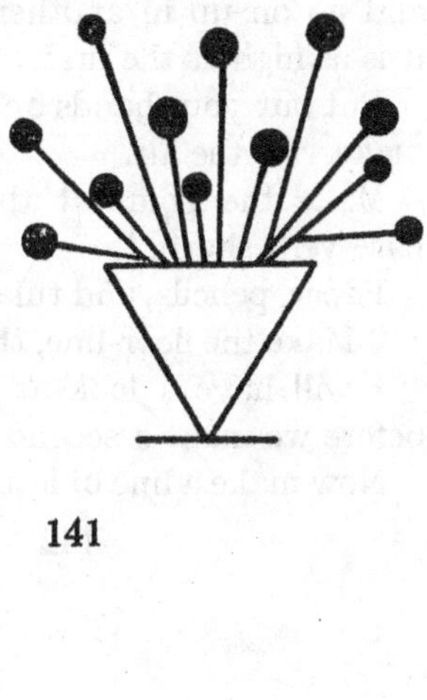

" It is **v**."

" **v** is a quiet letter. We do not make use of our voices when we say it, only of our lips and breath.

Everyone say **'vesl.**

Now say **v**-for-vessel.

See how the letter is like the picture.

Take the flowers from your stick picture, then take off the top of the vessel and the little foot.

Now you have the letter **v** in sticks.

Put back the apparatus.

See me make **v** on the blackboard.

Its foot is on the line, and it is as high as letter **i**.

I make a start at the top left-hand side. Down I go sloping to the right till I get to the floor-line. There I make a sharp turn and go on up in another sloping line till it is as high as the first.

Put out your hands and make **v** in the air.

Make the point at the base very sharp."

Paper, pencils, and rulers are given out.

" Make the floor-line, then make letter **v**.

I will have a look at everyone's letter before we make a second one.

Now make a line of letter **v's**.

Make them all equally high, and all with straight sloping sides and sharp points at the base."

The teacher goes round giving help.

For the less bright boys it will be a good idea to put three guiding points, one for the start, one for the turn, and one for the end. Take care that they get these joined in the right order.

Letter **v** seems a simple letter, but it is hard for small boys and girls to make.

*Word-building*

vessel

## 23

**w**$^{\text{ə}}$-for-worm

*Apparatus :*

(i) Plasticine.

(ii) White paper, pencils, and rulers.

The teacher puts the wall-card 'w' in front of the group.

" What is this picture?"

" It is a worm."

" A worm is a little animal living in the earth.

He is something like a snake, but much smaller, and he has no head and no poisoned bite.

He makes a deep, narrow hole in the earth, and at the end of this he has his house, lined with leaves and other soft things.

He keeps out of view as much as possible because the birds go after him whenever they see him.

He is light red in colour, and he goes about by twists and turns.

See me make a worm of Plasticine.

I make a long thin roll and get it bent up and down this way. Worms are able to put their bodies into all sorts of positions, but first we will make one like the one on the wall-card. It goes down, up, down, and up again.

Everyone say **wəːɹm** with care."

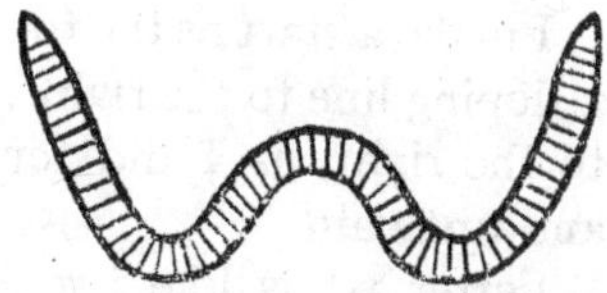

The Plasticine is now given out.

When they have all made two or three worms, the teacher again puts up the wall-card.

" Is anyone able to give the name of the letter in the picture?"

" It is **wᵊ**."

" Everyone say **wᵊ** for-worm.

See me make the twisting letter with my hands.

You do the same.

Put the tops of your two thumbs together and your fingers out to the sides.

Now do it the other way: with your fingers together and your thumbs out.

Now see me make the letter on the blackboard.

It has two pointed feet on the line, and is as tall as letter **i**.

I make a start at the top, and go down in a sloping line to the right ; then I come up to the right, as I did for **v** ; then down and up again.

Letter **w**ə is like two letter **v**'s joined together.

In the French language it is named ' two v's.'

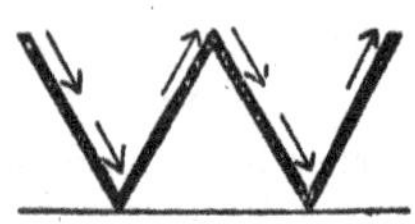

Put out your hands and we will make letter **w**ə in the air.

Everyone say **w**ə."

Paper, pencils, and rulers are given out.

" Make a floor-line and do a line of letter **w**ə's."

The teacher goes round giving help.

*Word-building*

wet went will well wind

**24**

**s**-for-snake

*Apparatus :*

(i) Finger-paints.

(ii) Pencils, white paper, and rulers.

The teacher takes down the wall-card 's' and puts it before the group.

"What is the picture?"

"It is a snake."

"There are a great number of different sorts of snakes.

It is quite safe to go near some of them, but some have poison in their bite, and some are strong enough to put a man to death by twisting themselves round him and crushing him in their folds.

Some are very brightly coloured and marked, and come from the woods in warm countries. Others are small and quiet in colour, and come from colder places. Snakes have no legs. They go forward by twisting and turning their long thin bodies.

The snake in the picture is going to take a bite of something. He has his body lifted from the earth to do so.

He is making the hissing sound 'ssss' which snakes make when they are angry.

Now you are all going to be snakes like the one in the picture.

Get on your knees on the floor and put your arms flat against your body as if you didn't have any.

Now put your head forward and make the ' ssss ' sound of an angry snake.

Go back to your seats.

Put out your hands and we will make the curves of the snake going forward on the floor. Up and down and up and down.

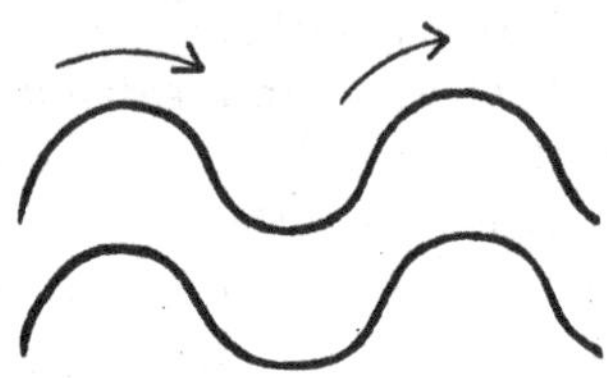

Now put your hands high up and we will make a great tall snake curving from side to side.

Make beautiful round curves, because snakes make very beautiful motions.

Now do this first with one hand and then with the other.

Now do the snake in the picture.

He has only two curves, first back, then forward."

These motions are kept up till the boys and girls are able to do them without trouble.

Then the finger-paints are given out.

" We are going to make snakes with paints.

You may take any colour and you may make your snakes short or long, but take care to give them all beautiful round curves. The snakes may be flat on the earth or up on their tails."

They do this till the curves are round and controlled. Then the papers are put up to get dry and the boys and girls go round to see one another's work.

" Everyone say **sneik** with care.

Now have a look at the wall-card again.

Is anyone able to say the name of the letter?"

" It is **s**."

" The letter is formed like the snake and it makes the same sound.

Everyone say **s**-for-snake.

**s** is not a simple letter to make and we will make it first without the floor-line.

See me do it on the blackboard.

First I make a letter **k**[e]-for-curve, but I do not take off the chalk. I go on and make another curve the other way round, turning back under the first.

Go to the blackboards and make letter **s**.

Make a great number of them, some great, some quite small. Let the top curve be the same size as the lower one."

When they are able to do this without trouble, they go to their seats, and white paper, pencils, and rulers are given out.

" Letter **s** is seated on the line on its tail.

See me do one on the blackboard.

I make a start high up with the **k**[a] curve, then round in the opposite direction, touching the floor-line on the way, and ending a little over it at the left.

Letter **s** would be more simple to make if it was a tall letter, but though it has such a number of curves it is no taller than letter **i**.

Do it in the air, and let the table be the floor-line.

Put your hands up high, and make a curve first to the left, then round to the right, giving the table a touch when you come round and up.

Now make a floor-line on your white paper, and make a line of letter **s**'s.

Take care to keep them all as high as one another."

The teacher goes round giving help.

*Word-building*

| | | | | |
|---|---|---|---|---|
| lets | send | sent | kiss | loss |
| rest | sand | self | silk | slip |
| step | stop | swim | test | twist |
| sock | stamp | stem | stick | stiff |
| mass | smell | dress | sad | mist |
| | sun | skin | soft | |

## 25

**j°-for-young**

*Apparatus :*

(i) Picture of a woman from the cold north with her baby.

(ii) Coloured chalks and blackboards.

(iii) White paper, pencils, and rulers.

" Today we are going to have a talk about the men and women of the cold north. Their houses are made of snow.

These small round houses of snow are not very warm, but they keep out the biting winds.

For food, those living in this cold country have the fish which they get from the water under the thick ice. Their clothing is made of the skins of animals.

Here is a picture of a woman from that land of ice and snow. See her skin clothing, and in the distance her little round house made of snow.

Do you see what she has on her back? It is a parcel. It is a baby in a parcel."

The teacher puts up the wall-card 'y.'

"Here is a clearer view of the baby in his parcel. It is like a bag with a hole at the top for the baby to see out. He has warm clothing round him, and seems very happy in his parcel.

Now go to your blackboards and make pictures of men and women living in the cold north, and be certain to make a picture of the baby in his parcel."

When they have all made pictures and gone round to see one another's work, they go back to their seats.

"You will not be able to give the name of the letter from what I have said, so give me all your attention.

The baby is young, and from the picture you see the way in which the mother takes her young one about.

Everyone say **jʌŋ**.

Now is anyone able to give the letter?"

" It is **jᵊ**."

" It is **jᵊ**-for-**jʌŋ**. Everyone say it.

Take another look and see in what way the picture is like the letter. It is the baby-parcel without the baby in it.

There is the hole at the top. There is the right side and there is the round base.

The other side, the left, is not there.

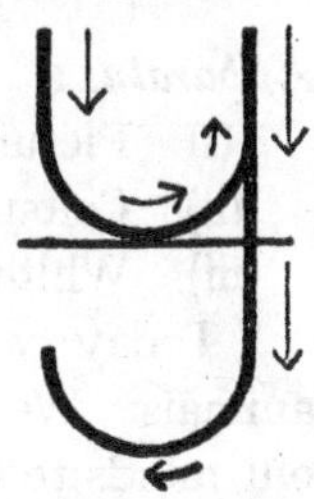

To make the letter we do the round part at the top first. Down and round and up we go, then straight down under the line, and round and up to the left.

At the start it is like letter **ʌ** but it has a tail like letter **gᵊ**.

See me do it on the blackboard."

The white paper, pencils, and rulers are given out.

" Make a floor-line and do a line of letter **jᵊ**'s. I will come round and give help."

*Word-building*

yes

## 26

## z-for-zebra

*Apparatus* :

(i) Pictures of animals.

(ii) Coloured chalks and blackboards.

(iii) White paper, pencils, and rulers.

" Today we are going to see some animals. We are going on a journey in our minds to a great field where a number of different animals are kept on view.

These animals are in great boxes with open fronts so that we are able to see in. Across these open fronts are strong iron rods to keep the animals from getting out, because some of them are strong and violent and would quickly make a meal of any small boy or girl.

The place where all these animals are to be seen is the animal gardens.

Here are pictures of animals at the animal gardens. Not all the animals are violent, and in England there is one of these Gardens where the quieter animals are not kept shut up, but are free to go walking about anywhere."

The pictures of animals are then given out and there is a general discussion of the animals.

The teacher takes care that the *zebra*[1] is given special attention.

"This beautiful animal is a zebra. He is a little like a small horse, but he has a very uncommon coat of yellow-white banded all over with black.

Everyone say **'ziːbrə.**

The zebra comes from the great grasslands of Africa. There he goes about all day in a group with other zebras, looking for grass for food, and at the same time taking care to keep out of the way of violent animals such as 'lions,' the great yellow-brown cats which are so strong that men say they are the Kings of the animals. These cats would quickly make a meal of a zebra. The zebras are helped by their

[1] An animal from Africa.

coats of black and white, because when they are quiet under the trees it is hard for the lions to see them. Their bands make them seem like the shade of the trees on the grass, with sunlight falling on it through the leaves.

In this picture one zebra is resting on the earth and the other is on his four feet."

The pictures of animals are then put away.

"Go to the blackboards and make pictures of some of the animals you would see in the animal gardens. Be certain to make a picture of a zebra in his black and white coat."

When the boys and girls have made some pictures they take another look at the wall-card 'z.'

"See, here are the two zebras. The one which is resting is like the letter under the picture. You do not see his four legs because they are under him.

See how his head and neck and body make the form of the letter. Is anyone able to say the name of the letter?"

"It is **z**."

"Everyone say **z**-for-zebra.

Now give the zebra's back a rub. Put

out your hand. It is on the zebra's nose. Let your hand go over his head, between his ears, make a sharp turn, and go down his neck, then make another sharp turn and go on to his tail.

The letter **z** is made in the same way: by giving the zebra a rub.

Put out your hands and we will make it in the air."

The pencils, papers, and rulers are now given out.

" See how I do letter **z**.

Letter **z**, like the zebra, is seated on the floor-line. It is as high as letter **i**.

Make a start at his nose, and go in a straight line to the right. Make a sharp turn, then go down in a sloping line to the left. When you get to the floor-line make another sharp turn and go straight on to the right.

See, if I make two more straight lines at the sides my letter becomes a square.

If the letter does not make a good square, it is badly made. Put out your hands and we will make **z** in the air.

Now make a floor-line and do a line of **z**'s on paper.

If you make one which is specially good, you may put in the two side lines and make it into a square.

I will come round and give you help, and see if you may make one of your **z**'s into a square."

27

**ks**-as-in-box

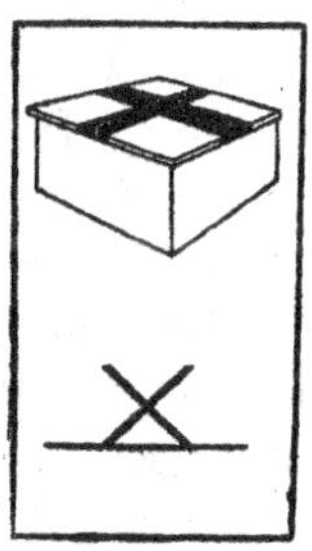

*Apparatus :*

(i) White paper, pencils, and rulers.

The teacher puts the wall-card '**x**' in front of the group.

" This is the last letter we have to do; and till we are learning very hard words we will come across **ks** only as the last letter of a word.

It is the last letter of the word 'box,'

the last letter of the word ' six,' and the last letter of the word ' wax.'

Is anyone able to say what it says?"

" It is **ks**."

" Everyone say **ks** with care.

Now say **boks**.

Have a look at the picture. It is the picture of a strange box with two tops. When one top is open and the other shut they make the form of letter **ks**.

Letter **ks** is a simple letter to make.

It is two sloping lines going across one another.

The letter has its two feet on the floor-line, and the lines go across one another at their middle points.

It is as high as letter **i**.

The two lines which make **ks** are made one after the other.

First we go down in a sloping line from left to right, stopping at the floor-line.

Then we take the chalk off, and, starting a little more to the right than before, we go down from right to left.

Put out your hands and we will do it in the air."

White paper, pencils, and rulers are given out.

" Make a floor-line and do a line of letter **ks**'s."

The teacher goes round giving help.

*Word-building*

box tax wax six

## PART IV

### MORE TRAINING IN LETTERS

When the letters have been taken one by one in the order given, it is necessary to go over them all again in their *abc* order. This second time the boys and girls are given the 'long name' of the letter, its form as a 'great letter,' and every Basic word having the letter in it which may be formed by building.

Statements are put on the blackboard in writing, or given out to the group on printed cards, or said slowly by the teacher, and the boys and girls have to make copies of them or take them down from hearing.

New, special words are given with every letter. In these words the letters do not have their normal sound-value, and so it is necessary to get the sound of the complete word fixed in the minds of the learner together with its printed form. These are named "learning words." The others, which may be put together from

ABCD
EFGHI
JKLM
NOPQ
RSTUV
WXYZ

the separate sounds as given in Part III, are named " building-words."

One or two of these learning-words are taken in every step, and these are all used a number of times on the story-card from which reading is done in the last part of the hour.

In the work which comes now, more time is given to reading than to writing, and it is necessary for the teacher herself to make certain that the writing is getting better every day. It is important for no errors or bad letters to be overlooked, and for the line of letters at the top of every bit of writing to be done with special care.

Time is given every day to writing statements. These statements may be taken from the story cards, or, better, made up by the boys themselves. Lined paper, that is paper with lines printed on it, may be used.

The word-lists and the stories on the reading-cards are gone through in the last part of every hour. It is important for everyone in the group to have a card. The boys are given time to go over the reading cards quietly by themselves before they do the reading in turn with the teacher. While they are waiting for their turn at reading they may do some writing.

It is necessary for the teacher to go over every part of the work with every boy in turn.

There are sometimes two or three different word-lists. When this is so, every boy gets one list only, and does his work with a group, every one of whom has a different list. After they have done their reading out loud from the first card, they make an exchange of cards till every boy has been over every card.

The work is given in two parts, A and B. These parts may be taken together, or at different times.

The material for the word-lists and reading-cards needed in Part IV is given all together at the end of it.

## 1

a—the

" Take white paper, pencils, and rulers.

Make a floor-line.

Put **tᵊ-hᵊ-e**

No one will be able to say what this word is, because the sound of it is not formed by building up the sounds of the letters.

In some words the sounds of the letters are changed, so putting them together will not give us the sound of the word, and we have to get the right way of saying those words into our heads by learning it.

Such words are given the name of 'learning-words.'

**t$^{ə}$-h$^{ə}$-e** is a learning-word and it says **ðə.**

Everyone say **ðə.**

Now put down in writing 'the cat'."

Everyone does this.

Word-list Ia is given out.

Everyone gets a card.

" Go through the words on your card quietly by yourselves.

Then do them in writing, but put 'the' before every word."

They are given a long bit of lined paper for this.

" You have all done the words putting 'the' in front of them.

Now we are going to do them again, with **ə** in front.

When we have to put '**ə** man,' or '**ə** bag,' we make use of letter **a.**

See me do '**ə** box' on the blackboard.

Now, on the other side of the paper, do some of the words again, putting **ə** before them."

## 2

'A'

**I.**

The teacher makes letter 'a' on the blackboard.

" What is that letter?"

" It is **a**."

" It has another name, a long name.

Sometimes it makes use of its long name in a word, and older persons give it the long name whenever they say the letter.

The long name is **ei**.

Everyone say **ei**.

In future we will give the letter **a** the name **ei** whenever we see it, but we have to keep in mind that it most commonly says **a**.

Make letter **ei** in the air with your two hands, then with one hand after the other.

Take white paper, pencils, and rulers, and make a floor-line.

Now make a line of letter 'a's.'

Now have a look at this new letter.

It is a 'great a.'

The 'a' on the wall-card is a 'small a.'

Every letter has a small form, which is the one you see most frequently, and a great form. This great letter has two uses. We have to put a great letter at the start of a statement, and we have to put one at the start of a person's name, such as Tom, and Ann, or the name of a town or country, such as Africa."

The teacher puts these names on the blackboard.

" All those first letters are great letters.

All great letters are the same size. They are as tall as letter **l**, and they all have their feet on the floor-line.

This is how we make great ' a.' Starting at the top, we make a sloping line down to the left ; then, from the top again, another sloping line down to the right. Then put the little line across the middle. It is half-way up.

Make a line of great ' a's.'

Get into groups of four."

The four word-lists for A are then given out to the groups, every boy in a group getting a different list.

" Go through the lists reading the words to yourselves, and come to me if you are unable to get the sound of any word.

When you have been through one list,

make an exchange of cards with someone in your group, till you have all had all the four lists. Then take your paper and pencils and do six of the words in your last list in writing.

If you have a word whose first letter is 'a' you may make it a great 'a.'"

**II.**

"We are going to put a statement in writing. A statement says something, and there are two things to keep in mind about it. It has to have a great letter at the start, and it has to have a full-stop at the end.

A full-stop is a small round point. You put it on the floor-line after the last letter of a statement.

I will put a statement on the black-board."

The teacher puts down "A man went up the steps."

"Will someone put a finger on the great letter?

Now someone put a finger on the full-stop.

Now we will take the words one after the other, and go through the statement to see what it has to say."

They do this together.

Then the boys put the statement down in writing.

" Now I am going to put up two new learning-words."

The teacher puts ' was ' and ' is ' on the blackboard.

" We will do the small word first.

If we did it by building we would get **is**, but the sound of this word is **iz**.

Letter **s** has become **z**. It frequently does this when it comes at the end of a word.

Everyone say **iz**.

The other word is harder.

Letter ' a ' in this word says **ɔ** and letter **s** says **z**.

The word is **wɔz**.

Everyone say **wɔz**."

Reading-card 1 is then given out.

" There are five statements on this card, and if you are able to make them out you will have a story.

You will see the two new learning-words at the top of your cards.

Go through them quietly by yourselves.

I will let everyone do the reading in turn.

While you are waiting for your turn, take your pencils and papers and put down two statements from your reading card, one with the word ' was ' in it and one with the word ' is '."

3

' B '

**I.**

The teacher makes the letter ' b ' on the blackboard.

" What is that letter?"

" It is **b**$^{ə}$."

" It's long name is **biː** but it never says anything but **b**$^{ə}$.

Everyone say **biː**.

Make it in the air.

Now make a line of ' b's.'

The great letter ' b ' is hard.

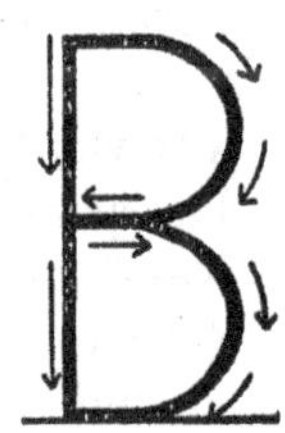

First you make a line like letter **l**. Then, starting at the top of the line, you make a half-circle to the right, coming back to the line in the middle, and, without taking the chalk off, you go on and make another half-circle under the first. The two half-circles are the same size and the lower one is resting on the floor line.

Make it in the air two or three times.

Now make a line of great ' b's '."

Word-lists B are then given out to groups of three.

" Go over the words quietly, then do some in writing.

If you have a word which has ' b ' for its first letter you may make a great ' b '."

**II.**

Reading-card 2 is given out.

" We have three new learning-words.

The first one has the same name as its first letter. It is **bi:**.

Say it.

The word after it is **put.**

Everyone say it.

Is anyone able to give me the sound of the third word?"

" It is **put** with an **s** on the end."

" It is **puts** . All say it.

Go through your reading, and while you are waiting to come to me put some statments in writing.

Give one statement with ' put ' in it and one with ' be '."

The use of the ''s' is pointed out to every boy when he does his reading with the teacher.

# 4

## ‘C’

**I.**

The teacher puts a letter **‘c’** on the blackboard.

“What is that letter?”

“It is **kə**-for-curve.”

“It has a long name; its long name is **siː**.”

Everyone say **siː**.

Take your pencils and do a line of letter ‘c’s.’

The great ‘c’ has the same form as the small ‘c,’ but it is twice the size.

Do a line of great ‘c’s’.”

Word-lists C are then given out, and a long bit of lined paper.

“Get in groups of three for the lists.

Go over the lists quietly, then do one list in writing. If you have a word with ‘c’ for its first letter, you may make a great ‘c’.”

**II.**

Reading-card **3** is then given out.

“We have four new learning-words at the top of the reading-card; two are very like one another, and when we have got one the other will not be hard.

The first one is **kʌm.**

Everyone say **kʌm.**

Now is anyone able to say the other word? It is **kʌm** with **s** on the end."

" It is **kʌmz.**"

" The third one is **keim**; and the last one is **tuː.**

Say **keim** and put your finger on the word.

Say **tuː** and put your finger on the word.

Now do your reading, and for your writing while you are waiting your turns, put down one statement with ' come ' in it, and one with ' comes.'

**5**

**' D '**

**I.**

The teacher puts the letter ' d ' on the blackboard.

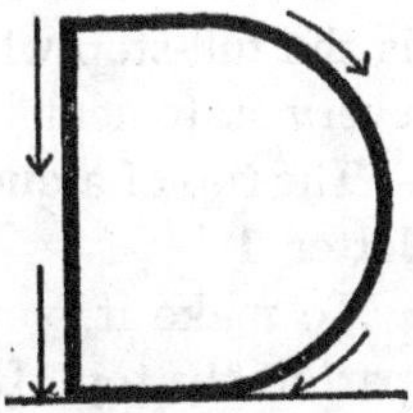

" What is that letter?"

" It is **d.**"

" Its long name is **diː** but it says **d** wherever you see it.

Everyone say **di:**.

Put out your hands and make ' d ' in the air.

Now take pencils and paper and make a line of ' d's.'

Now have a look at the great ' d.'

First we make a line like a letter **l**. Then, starting at the top, we make a half circle to the right, joining the straight line again at its foot.

Do it in the air.

Now do a line of great ' d's ' on paper."

When they have done this the teacher makes a question-mark on the blackboard.

" What is that strange thing?"

With the help of the teacher they make the discovery that it is a question-mark.

" We put a question-mark at the end of a question.

Any words which put a question have a question-mark at the end.

The little mark under the strange curve is the full-stop which comes at the end of every statement.

The top of a question-mark is as high as letter **l**

To make it, you first make the curved part at the top. It is a ' c ' made the other way round. Then you go down in a little straight line.

Last of all put in the full-stop.

Make a question mark in the air.

Now say **'kwestʃn maːrk.**

Take your pencils and paper and make a line of question-marks."

Word-lists D are now given out.

" Get in groups of three for your word-lists. Go over them with one another and put one of them in writing."

**II.**

Reading-card 4 is given out.

" Have a look for a question-mark on your reading-card.

When you see one, put your finger on it and I will come round and say if you are right.

Now take a look at the two new learning-words.

The little word is **duː**. Everyone say **duː.**

The other word is **dʌz**. Everyone say **dʌz.**

There are statements on your cards with these two words in.

Go through the cards by yourselves, then do some writing.

Put ' do ' and ' does ' into your writing.

Make up a statement with these words in it and put it down."

## 6

‘ E ’

**I.**

The teacher puts the letter ‘ e ’ on the blackboard.

" What is that letter?"

" It is **e**."

" Put out your hands and do it in the air.

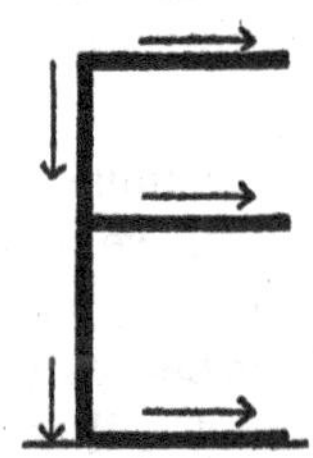

Its long name is **iː** Everyone say **iː**.

Now do a line of ‘ e’s ’ on paper.

This is the great ‘ e.’

It is made of four straight lines. One is like letter **l**. Then there are three others coming from its right side, one from the top, one from the middle, and one from the foot. We make the top one first and the lowest one last.

Make some great ‘ e’s ’ in the air.

Now do a line of them on paper."

Word-lists E are then given out.

" Get into groups of four and go over the lists. Everyone put one list into writing."

**II.**

Reading-card **5** is given out.

" We have three learning-words, all short ones.

Letter ' e ' sometimes makes use of its long name in words. It has done this in the first two words.

The first word is **hiː**. Everybody say **hiː**.

The second word is **ʃiː**. Everybody say **ʃiː**.

The last word is not hard. The sound of letter **f** here is softer than its common sound.

The word is **ɔv**. Everyone say **ɔv**.

Now do your reading and writing.

Put down any statement from the card, or make one up."

## 7

### ' F '

**I.**

The teacher makes the letter ' f ' on the blackboard.

" What is that letter?"

" It is **f**."

" Its long name is **ef** but it most frequently says **f**."

Make it in the air and say **ef** while you are doing so.

Do a line of ' f's ' in writing.

Here is the great ' f,' and this is how to make it.

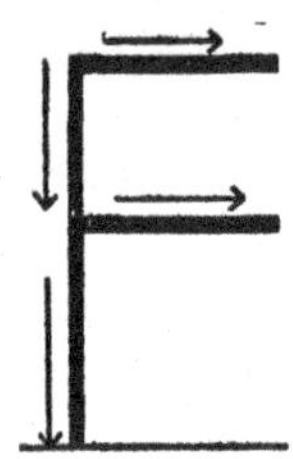

First make a line like letter **l.**

Then make the two side lines to the right.

Do the top one first.

The second one is at the middle of the **l** line.

Make great ' f ' in the air.

Do a line of great ' f's ' in writing.

Get in groups of two for the lists."

Word-lists F are given out.

" Go over the words and come to me for help.

Put one of the lists into writing."

**II.**

Reading-card 6 is given out.

" You have two new learning-words.

The first one is **fɔː*r*.**

Put your finger on the word and say **fɔ*r*.**

The other word is **'eibl.**

Put your finger on it and say **'eibl.**

Do your reading quietly and I will take you in turn.

For writing make up one statement with the word ' able ' in it and another with the word ' for.'

## 8

### ' G '

**I.**

The teacher puts the letter ' g ' on the blackboard.

" What is that letter?"

" It is letter **g**."

" Do it in the air.

Its long name is **dʒiː**.

Everyone say **dʒiː**.

Now do a line of letter 'g's ' on paper.

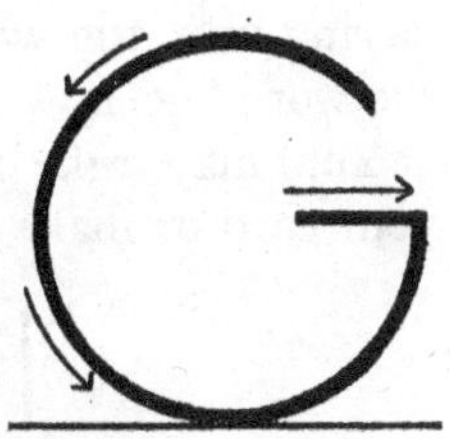

This is its great form. First a great ' c,' then a small line across the turned-up end.

Do it in the air.

Now do a line of great ' g's ' on paper."

Word-lists G are given out.

" Get into twos and go over the lists, and come to me for help.

Then do a list in writing, putting great ' g's ' wherever possible."

II.

Reading-card 7 is given out.

" We have three new words.

The first one is **gou.**

Everyone put a finger on it and say **gou.**

The second is **gouz.**

Put a finger on it and say **gouz.**

The last one is **gɔn.**

Put a finger on it and say it.

Now do your reading, and I will take you in turn.

For writing, do two statements, one having in it the word ' go ' and the other the word ' goes.'

You may take these statements from your card or make them up."

**9**

' H '

I.

The teacher puts the letter ' h ' on the blackboard.

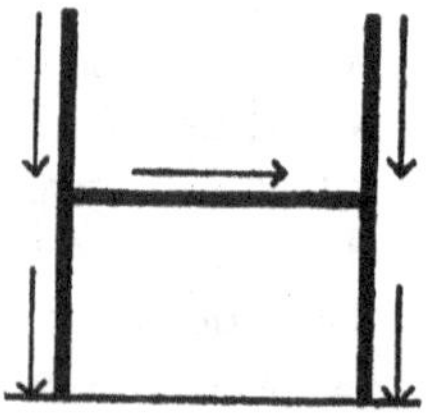

"What is this letter?"

" It is letter **h.**"

" Put out your hands and make it in the air.

Its long name is **eitʃ.**

Everyone say **eitʃ**.

Do a line of 'h's' on paper.

The great 'h' is very simple. Two lines like letter **l** and a joining-line across.

We do the two tall lines first, and put the line across half-way up.

Make great 'h's' in the air.

Do a line of great 'h's' on paper."

Word-lists H are given out.

"Go over the lists quietly and come to me for help.

Do some words in writing."

**II.**

Reading-card **8** is given out.

We have two new words.

The first one is **hav**. Everyone put their finger on it and say **hav**.

The other one is **həːr**. Everyone put their finger on it and say it.

Go over your cards quietly and I will take you for reading in turn.

While you are waiting, put down two statements in writing, one with 'have' in it and the other with 'her'."

## 10

### ‘ I ’

**I.**

The teacher makes letter ‘ i ’ on the blackboard.

“ What is that letter?”

“ It is letter **i**.”

“ Its long name is **ai**. Everyone say **ai**.

Do it in the air with your hands.

Now do a line of letter ‘ i’s ’ on paper.

This is the great ‘ i.’ It is a very simple letter.

It is the same size and form as letter **l** but with a small line across the top and another across the foot, which is on the floor-line.

Do it in the air.

First the tall straight line, then the little top line, then the one at the foot.

Do a line of great ‘ i’s ’.”

Word-lists I are given out.

“ Get in groups of four and go over the lists. Come to me for help if you have any trouble.

Put one list in writing.”

II.

Reading-card 9 is given out.

" We have here four new words.

The first one is the great ' i ' by itself.

That is the word we make use of when we are talking of ourselves.

Whenever ' i ' is used as a word we make a great ' i.'

The other two words are not hard. They are almost building-words, but the ' e's ' at the end make no sound.

The first is **giv.**

In the second, letter ' a ' says its long name. It is **geiv.**

Say them, putting a finger on them at the same time. The last one is **givz.** Everyone say **givz.**

Get on quietly and I will take you for reading in turn.

For writing, put down any statement."

## 11

## 'J'

I.

The teacher puts the letter ' j ' on the blackboard.

" What is that letter?"

" It is letter **dz.**"

" Its long name is **dzei**, but it never says anything but **dz.**"

Everyone say **dzei** and make the letter in the air with your hands.

Now do a line of letter ' **j**'s ' on paper.

This is great ' **J.**'

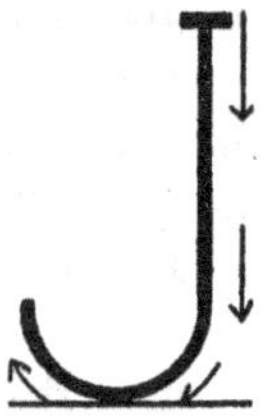

Starting at the top, we go almost to the floor-line. Then we go round in a half-circle to the left, down to the floor-line, and up again. Lastly we put a small line across the top.

Do it in the air.

Now do a line of great ' **J**'s.'

Now take down a word : **dz-ʌ-m-p.**

Is anyone able to say what the word is?"

" It is ' jump '."

" Do it again, this time with a great ' J '."

There are no word-lists for this letter.

**II.**

Reading-card 10 is given out.

" The two new words are not hard.

When two letter ' e's ' come together they say **iː** and we saw before that letter **s** frequently says **z** when it comes at the end of a word.

Keeping these rules in mind, by building up the two words we get **si :** and **si:z.**

Say the words, and put your finger on the right word when you do so.

Now do your reading quietly, and come to me in turn.

For writing, put down one statement with ' see ' in it, and one with ' sees '."

## 12

### ' K '

**I.**

The teacher makes letter ' k ' on the blackboard.

" What is that letter ?"

" It is **k**-for-kick."

" Its long name is **kei** but it never says anything but **k**.

Everyone say **kei** and make it in the air.

Do a line of letter ' k's ' in writing.

This is great ' k.'

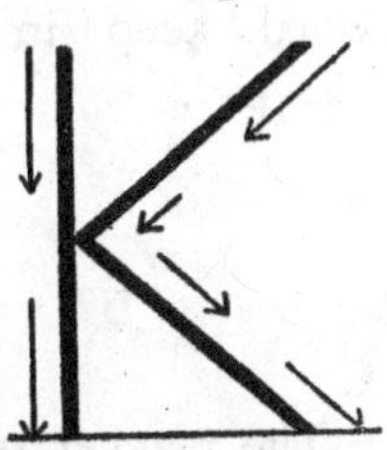

First we do the tall straight line. Then we do the two other lines in the same direction as for small ' k,' but this time we make our start opposite the top of the straight line, and the sharp turn is half-way down it.

Do great 'k' in the air.

Now do a line of great 'k's' on paper."

Word-lists K are then given out.

" Get in groups of three and go over the words, coming to me for help if you are in trouble.

Put a list in writing; if you come to a word starting with 'k,' make a great 'k'."

**II.**

Reading-card 11 is given out.

" The two new words are not hard.

Keep in mind that two 'e's' together say **iː**.

The two words are **kiːp** and **kiːps**.

Put your finger on them and say which is which.

Do your reading, and I will give you help in turn.

For writing, do one statement with the word 'keep' in it and one with the word 'keeps'."

**13**

'L'

**I.**

The teacher puts the letter 'l' on the blackboard.

" What is that letter?"

" It is letter **l**."

" Its long name is **el**, but it never says anything but **l**

Everyone say **el** and do it in the air.

Now make a line of 'l's' on paper.

This is great 'l.'

It is like the leg and foot.

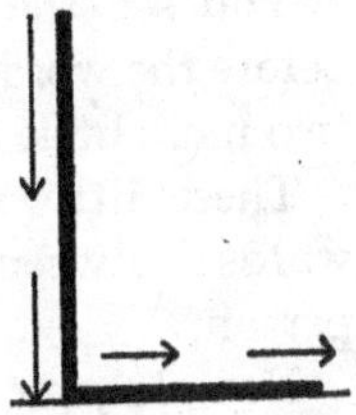

We make the tall bit first, then make a turn at the floor-line, and do the bit which is resting on it.

Do it in the air.

Now do a line of great 'l's' on paper."

Word-lists L are then given out.

" Get in groups of four and go over the words, coming to me for help if necessary.

Put a list in writing, making one great 'l'."

**II.**

Reading-card 12 is given out.

" We have three new words.

The first one is **sei.**

Letter 'a' here has its long name, and letter **j** is quiet.

The second is **sez.**

The last one is **sed.**

Put your finger on **sei** and say it.

Put your finger on **sez** and say it.

Put your finger on **sed** and say it.

You see the two little marks high up before the words said by Bob and Ben, and two more little marks at the end of them.

These little marks are a sign that the words between them are said by some person.

Now do your reading, and come to me in turn.

For writing, put down from your cards any statement which is said by someone.

Then you will be able to put in the little ' talk-marks '."

## 14

### ' M '

I.

The teacher puts the letter ' m ' on the blackboard.

" What is that letter?"

" It is letter **m.**"

" Its long name is **em** but it makes the sound **m** wherever it is.

Make it in the air and say **em.**

Now do a line of ' m's ' on paper.

This is the great ' m '.

It is hard to make.

First we make the tall line at the left side, starting at the top. Then we take off the chalk and put it on at the top again. We go sloping down to the right till we are half-way to the floor-line, then sloping up again till we are as high as our starting-point, then straight down to the floor-line.

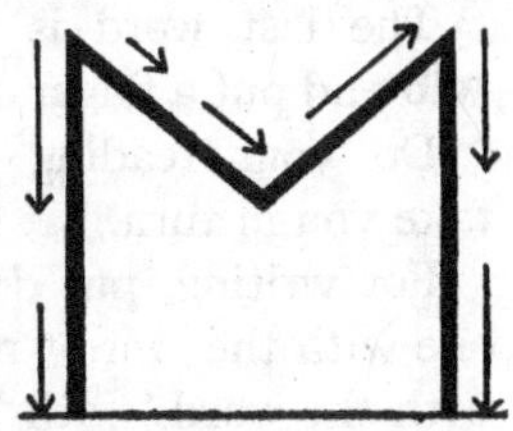

Make it in the air.

Now make a line of great ' m's' on paper."

Word-lists M are then given out.

" Get in groups of two and go over the lists, coming to me if you are in need of help.

Do one list in writing, making one or more great ' m's '."

**II.**

Reading-card 13 is given out.

" We have four new words.

In the first three, letter ' a ' says its long name, and letter ' e ' says nothing.

So we get **meid**, and **meik**, and **meiks**.

Say the three words, putting your finger on the one you are saying.

The last word is **wið**. Everyone say **wið** and put a finger on the word.

Do your reading quietly, and I will take you in turn.

For writing, put down two statements, one with the word 'make' in it, and one with the word 'with'."

## 15

### 'N'

**I.**

The teacher makes the letter 'n' on the blackboard.

" What is that letter?"

" It is letter **n**."

" Its long name is **en** but its sound is **n** wherever it is.

Make it in the air and say **en** while you are doing so.

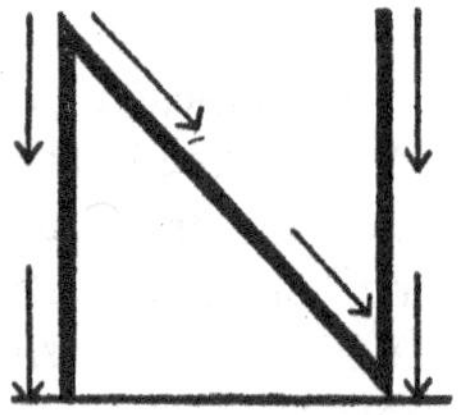

Make a line of letter 'n's' on paper.

This is the great 'n.'

It is three straight lines.

We make the left one first, like an ' l;' then the line across, sloping from the top of the first to the floor-line; and lastly another ' l,' meeting the floor-line at the same point.

Do it in the air.

Then make a line of great ' n's ' on paper."

They get into groups of four for the word-lists, and lists N are given out.

" Go over your lists, and I will come round giving help.

Put one in writing."

**II.**

Reading-card 14 is given out.

" You have two new words.

The first one is **teik** and the other is **tuk.**

Everyone say **teik** and put a finger on the word.

Now say **tuk** and put a finger on it.

Do your reading quietly first, then come to me in turn.

While you are waiting, put two statements in writing, one with the word ' takes ' in it and one with the word ' took '."

The teacher puts these two words on the blackboard.

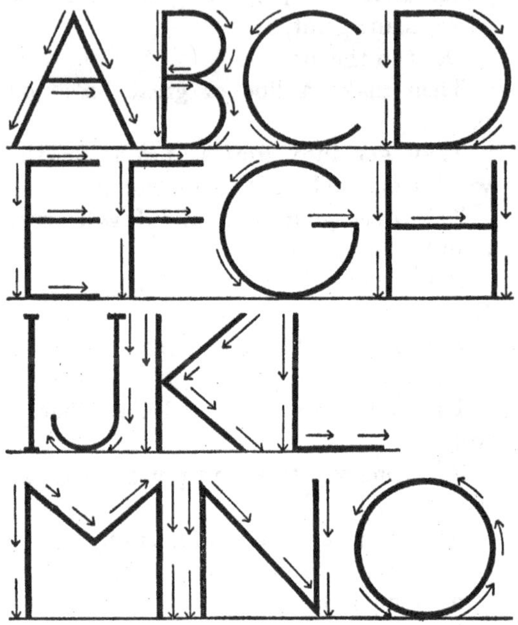
ABCD
EFGH
IJKL
MNO

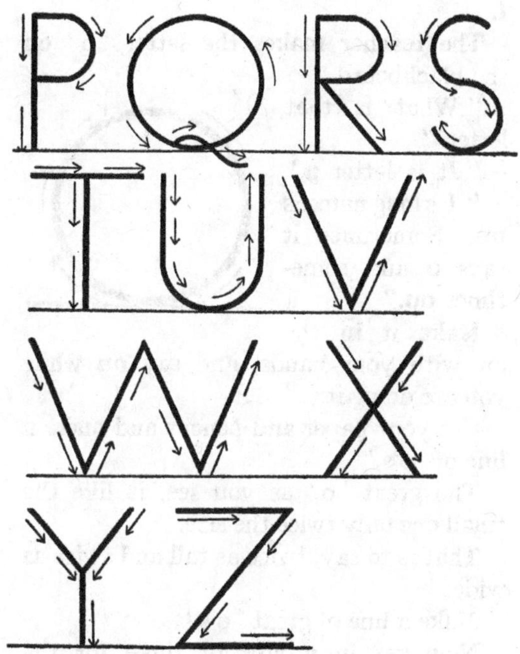


G

## 'O'

I.

The teacher makes the letter 'o' on the blackboard.

"What is that letter?"

"It is letter ɔ."

"Its long name is **ou**. Sometimes it says ɔ and sometimes **ou**."

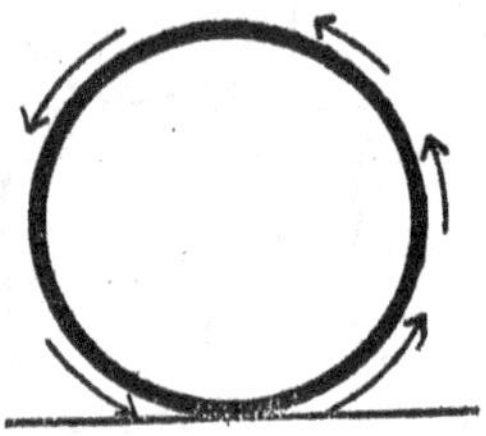

Make it in the air with your hands, and say **ou** while you are doing it.

Get your paper and pencils and make a line of 'o's.'

The great 'o,' as you see, is like the small one only twice the size.

That is to say, twice as tall and twice as wide.

Make a line of great 'o's.'

Now get in groups of three for the lists."

Lists O are given out.

"Go over the words with one another, and I will come round and give you help.

Put down one list in writing."

II.

Reading-card 15 is given out.

" You have three new words.

The first one is **mei** and the last one is **tiː**.

Put your finger on **tiː** and say it. Now say **mei** and put your finger on it.

The middle word you will be able to do by building if you keep in mind that the ' h ' here is quiet and makes no sound.

What is the word?"

" It is **wen**."

" Everyone say **wen** and put a finger on it.

Go on with your reading, and come to me in turn.

For writing, do one statement with ' may ' in it, and one with ' when '."

## 17

' P '

I.

The teacher puts the letter ' p ' on the blackboard.

" What is this letter?"

" It is letter **p**."

" Its long name is **piː** but its sound is **p** at all times.

Make it in the air and say **pi:**.

Now do a line of letter ' p's ' on paper.

Great ' p ' is very like small ' p,' but it has its foot on the line.

We do not make it as we make the small ' p '.

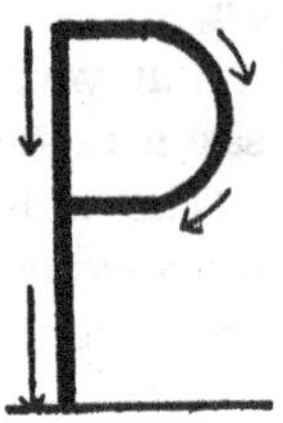

We make first the tall ' l ' at the left, then, starting again from the top, we go round in a half-circle to the right, coming back to the l-line half-way down.

Do it in the air with your hands.

Now do a line of great ' p's ' in writing."

Lists P are now given out.

" Get in groups of three for the word-lists.

Go over them with one another, and come to me for help.

Put one list in writing."

II.

Reading-card 16 is given out.

" You have three learning-words.

The first one is **mi:** and the last one is **mai**.

Say **mai** and put your finger on the word.

Now say **mi:** and put your finger on it.

The middle word is **gud**.

Say **gud** and put a finger on it.

Go on with your reading quietly. Then come to me in turn.

For writing, put down a statement with the word ' good ' in it, and one which has ' give ' for its first word.

Take these statements from your cards."

## 18

'Q'

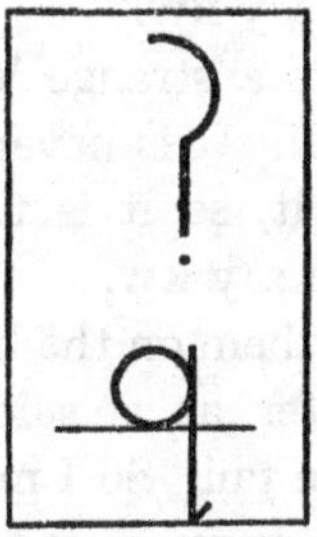

I.

" Today we are going to take a new letter, that is, one we have not had before.

The letter is something like a question-mark.

I will make it on the blackboard.

It is seated on the floor-line with a tail which goes under.

It is very like letter ' g ' in form; the only thing which is different is its tail.

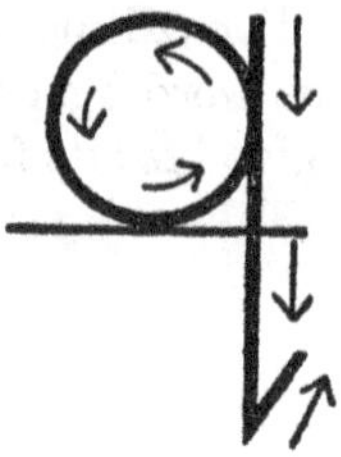

This is pointed, not curved, and goes to the right and not to the left.

Have a look at the question-mark again. See the curve and the tail. Is anyone able to give the name of this letter?"

" It is **kw.**"

" Everyone say **kw.**"

Letter **kw** is a strange letter. It is of no use by itself. It is never seen without letter ʌ after it, so it is the two letters together which say **kw.**

I will make them on the blackboard.

The new letter, as we said, is like letter ' **g** ' all but the tail. So I make letter ' g ' till I get to the curve in its tail.

Then in place of making a curve, I make a sharp turn and go up a little way to the right.

You are all able to make letter ʌ.

Put out your hands and make in the air the two letters which together say **kw.**

Now do a line of them on paper. Keep

the two letters near to one another, but make a space between the groups."

**II.**

" Now this new letter like the question-mark has a long name like the others.

Its name is **kjuː**.

Everyone say **kjuː**.

The great ' q ' is like great ' O ' putting its tongue out.

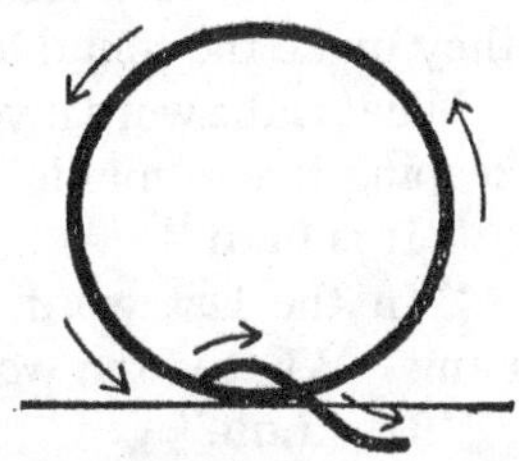

We make the ' O ' part first.

Then we put in the tongue.

Put out your hands and make great ' q ' in the air, saying **kjuː** while you are doing it.

Make a line of great ' q's.'

The **kw** sound, that of ' q ' and ʌ together, is not very common, and I have only one word to give you.

I will give you the letters of the word. Take them down while I am saying them.

First the two letters which together make **kw** that is qʌ.

Now ' i,' ' c,' and ' k.'

What is the word?"

" It is ' quick '."

" Make it again, this time with a great 'q.'

Now make up, and put in writing, a statement with the word ' quick ' in it."

**III.**

Reading-card 17 is given out.

" There are three new words.

We will do the middle one first.

When letters **t** and h come together they make the sound **ð**.

What is the word if you do it by building, keeping this in mind?"

" It is **ðem**."

" In the last word, letter ' o ' says its name. What is the word, then?"

" It is **nou**."

" Everyone say **nou**."

The first word you will not be able to do by building.

It is **ðei**.

Everyone say **ðei** and put a finger on the word.

Now do your reading quietly, and I will take you in turn.

For writing, put down any statement from your reading-cards."

# 19

## 'R'

I.

The teacher makes letter 'r' on the blackboard.

" What is that letter?"

" It is **r**."

" Its long name is **aːr**."

Make it in the air and say **aːr** while you are doing so.

Now make a line of 'r's' on paper.

Here is the great 'r.'

It is like great 'p' with a long, straight tail.

To make it we first make a great 'p,' then we go on and do the tail down to the floor-line.

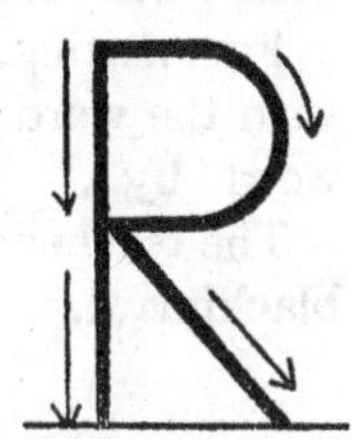

Make it in the air.

Now make a line of great 'r's' on paper."

Lists R are now given out.

" Get into groups of two for the lists.

Go over the words with one another, and I will give you help.

Put down one list in writing."

II.

Reading-card 18 is given out.

" You have three new learning-words.

The first one says the name of the letter we did last. It is **aːr**.

Everyone say it, and put a finger on the word.

The second we may do by building if we keep in mind that letter ' e ' sometimes says its name.

The word is **wiː**. Put your finger on it and say it.

The last word is **bai**.

Everyone say **bai** and put a finger on the word.

Do your reading by yourselves first, and then I will take you in turn.

For writing, put down one statement with the word ' are ' in it and one with the word ' by '."

The teacher puts these two words on the blackboard.

## 20

' S '

I.

The teacher puts the letter ' s ' on the blackboard.

" What is that letter?"

" It is letter **s**."

" Its long name is **es**."

Sometimes at the end of a word, as you saw, it says **z**, but generally it says **s**.

If it has another ' s ' with it, as in the words ' mass ' and ' across,' it makes the sound **s** even at the end of a word.

Make it in the air and say **es**.

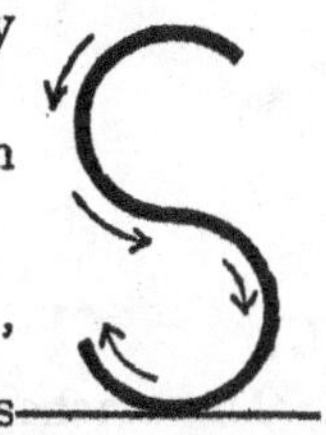

Make a line of ' s's ' on paper.

This is the great ' s.'

It is like the small ' s ' only twice as great. It is twice as tall and twice as wide.

Make a line of great ' s's ' on paper."

Lists S are now given out.

" Get in groups of three for the lists.

Go over the words together and come to me for help.

Put one list in writing."

**II.**

Reading-card 19 is given out.

" You have three new learning-words.

The first one is **juː**, and the second one is **juə*r***.

The last one is **aut**.

Say **juː** and put your finger on it.

Say **juər** and put your finger on it.

Say **aut** and put your finger on it.

Do your reading by yourselves first, and then I will take you in turn.

For writing, put down two statements, one with the word ' your ' in it, and one with the word ' out '."

## 21

### ' T '

**I.**

The teacher puts the letter ' t ' on the blackboard.

" What is that letter?"

" It is **t**."

" Its long name is **ti :** but it never says it.

It makes the sound **t** everywhere but where the letter **h** comes after it.

What sound do **ti:** and **h** make ?"

Together they say **ð**.

" We have had an example of that in ' the.' Other words of the same sort are ' this ' and ' that.'

Say **ti:** and make the letter in the air.

Now do a line of ' t's ' on paper.

Here is the great ' t.'

It is only two straight lines.

Make the tall one first.

Then put the line across the top from left to right.

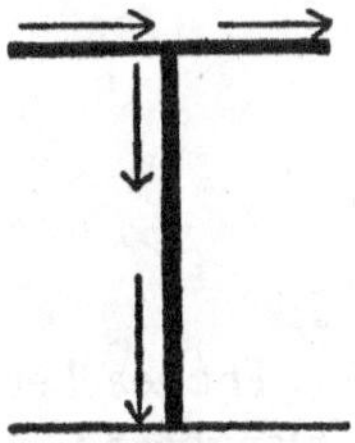

Make great ' t ' in the air.

Now do a line of great ' t's ' on paper.

Letter ' t ' is a very common letter. It is in a great number of words, and today you are going to have six lists."

Lists T are now given out.

" Get in groups of six and go over the words, coming to me for help.

Put one list in writing."

**II.**

Reading-card 20 is given out.

" You have two new learning-words.

The first one is **wɔt** and the other is **wai**.

Say **wai** and put your finger on it.

Now say **wɔt** and put your finger on that.

Do your reading, and I will take you one by one.

For writing, put down one statement with ' what ' in it, and one with ' why.'

22

'U'

I.

The teacher makes the letter 'u' on the blackboard.

"What is that letter?"

"It is **ʌ**."

"Its long name is **juː**.

Sometimes it says **ʌ** and sometimes **u**.

Make it in the air, and say **juː**.

Now do a line of 'u's' on paper.

The great 'u' is like the small 'u' but without the line by its side.

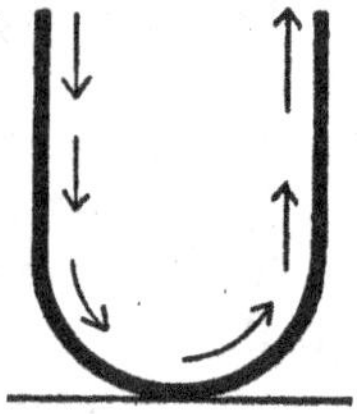

We make a start at the top left-hand side, then go down, round and up.

Do it in the air.

Now do a line on paper."

Lists U are now given out.

"Get in groups of two for the lists.

Go over the words with one another, and come to me for help.

Put one of the lists in writing."

II.

Reading-card 21 is given out.

" There are three new learning-words.

You will see that the last three letters of all three words are the same.

They are e, r, e.

The middle word is **ðeər** and the last word is **weər**.

Is anyone able to say what the first one is?"

" It is **heər**."

" Not quite. It is **hiər**, which is almost the same. Say **hiər**.

Do your reading quietly, and I will take you in turn.

For writing, put down two statements. You may take them from the card or make them up."

**23**

'V'

I.

The teacher makes letter 'v' on the blackboard.

" What is that letter?"

" It is v."

" Its long name is **viː**, but it never says anything but **v**.

Make it in the air and say **viː**.

Now do a line of letter ' v's ' on paper.

The great ' v ' is the same in form as the small ' v,' but twice the size.

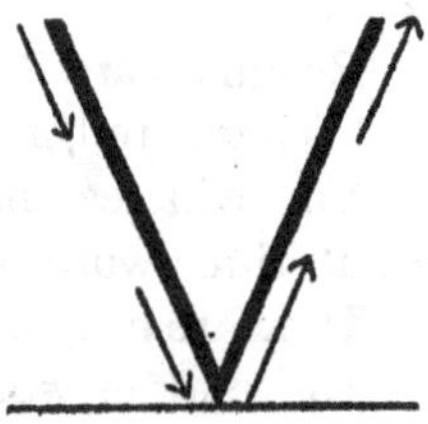

Make a start at the top of the left slope. Go down to the floor-line, then up the right slope.

Make great ' v ' in the air.

Make a line of great ' v's ' in writing.

Letter ' v ' is not a common letter, and we have only a small number of words with it in.

I will put one on the blackboard."

The teacher puts up the word ' vessel.'

" What is that word?"

" It is **'vesl**."

" Put it in writing."

**II.**

Reading-card 22 is given out.

" The first learning-word is **ˈeni** and the other is **sʌm**."

Say **sʌm** and put your finger on it.

Now say **ˈeni** and put your finger on it.

Go through the reading, and I will go over it with you in turn.

For writing, put down one statement with 'any' in it, and one with 'some'."

**24**

'W'

I.

The teacher makes the letter '**w**' on the blackboard.

"What is that letter?"

"It is letter **w**."

"Its long name is **'dʌbljuː**."

Make it in the air and say **'dʌbljuː**.

Now do a line of 'w's' on paper.

The great form of '**w**' is like the small one, but twice the size.

It is made in the same way as a small 'w.'

Do it in the air.

Make a line of great 'w's' on paper.

You will all have the same word-list today, so there will be no groups."

Word-list W is given out.

"Go over the words and come to me if you are in need of help.

Put your list in writing."

II.

Reading-card **23** is given out.

" The first learning-word is **'ounli**."

Put your finger on it and say **'ounli**.

The other word is **'ouvər**.

Put your finger on it and say **'ouvər**.

Do your reading quietly, then come to me in turn.

For writing, put down one statement with the word ' only ' in it and one with the word ' over '."

25

' X '

**I.**

The teacher puts the letter ' x ' on the blackboard.

" What is that letter?"

" It is **ks**."

" Its long name is **eks**, but its sound is **ks** wherever it is.

Make it in the air and say **eks**.

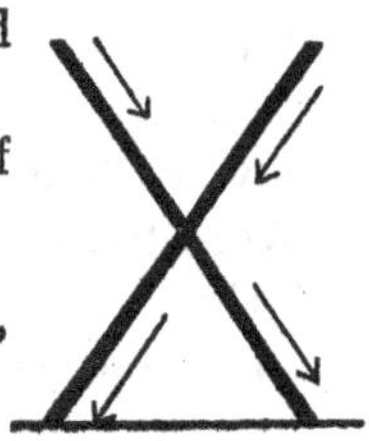

Now make a line of ' x's ' on paper.

Here is the great ' x.'

It is like the small ' x ' but twice the size.

Make it in the air.

Now do a line of great ' x's ' in writing.

There are five words with ' x ' in them, which we may do by building."

The teacher puts ' six,' ' tax,' ' wax,' ' box,' and ' sex ' on the blackboard.

The group do the building together.

" Now put these words on paper."

**II.**

Reading-card 24 is given out.

" You have two new words.

The first one is **huː**.

Put your finger on it and say **huː**.

The other word is **sou**.

Put your finger on it and say it.

Do your reading, and I will take you in turn.

For writing, make up one statement which has the word ' who ' in it, and one which has the word ' so '."

## 26

' Y '

**I.**

The teacher makes the letter ' y ' on the blackboard.

" What is that letter?"

" It is **j**."

" Its long name is **wai** and it has two sounds : sometimes it says **i** and sometimes **j**.

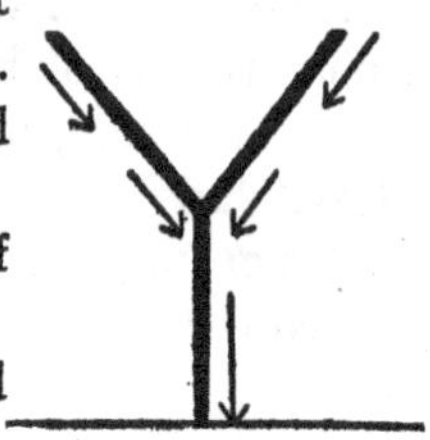

Do it in the air and say **wai**.

Now do a line of letter ' y's ' on paper.

The great ' y ' is hard to make.

Starting at the top left side, go in a sloping line to the right, half-way down to the floor-line.

Make a new start at the top right side, and go down to the end of the first line, then make a turn and go straight down to the floor-line.

Make it in the air.

Now make a line of great ' y's ' on paper."

**II.**

Reading-card 25 is given out.

" The two new words are not hard.

In the first one letter ' a ' says **aː**.

The word is **laːst**.

In the other one, letter ' y ' says **i**.

The word is **'veri**.

Go on with your reading, and I will take it with you in turn.

For writing, put down two statements, one with the word ' very ' in it and one with the word ' last.'

## 27

## ' Z '

**I.**

The teacher makes the letter ' z ' on the blackboard.

" What is that letter?"

" It is **z.**"

" Its long name is **zed** but it says **z** wherever it is.

Put out your hands and make the letter in the air, saying **zed** while you do so.

Do a line of letter ' z's ' on paper.

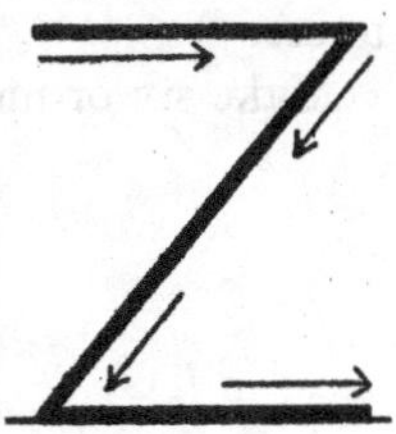

The great ' z ' has the same form as the small ' z ' but it is twice the size.

It is made in the same way as the small ' z.'

Do it in the air.

Now make a line of great ' z's.'

' z ' is not a common letter and there is no example in our lists."

**II.**

Reading-card 26 is given out.

" You have three new learning-words.

The first one is **'litl**, the second **mu:v,** and the last **ould.**

Say **mu:v** and put your finger on the word.

Say **'litl** and put your finger on the word.

Say **ould** and put your finger on the word.

Go through your reading and I will take you in turn.

For writing, every one of you make a copy of your names.

You have to put two great letters, one for the first letter of your first name, and one for the first letter of your second name.

Make six or more copies of your name."

MATERIAL FOR USE WITH PART IV.

(The word-lists and stories for use in connection with the same letter are grouped together, but are to be put on different cards. Words **in** black are to be printed on the cards in red.)

**1a**

| 1 | 2 |
|---|---|
| land | flag |
| man | hand |
| plant | hat |
| tax | rat |
| ant | stamp |
| bag | crack |
| band | mass |

---

A

| 1 | 2 | 3 | 4 |
|---|---|---|---|
| A | A | A | A |
| am | act | plant | bag |
| had | back | sand | band |
| at | crack | tax | cat |
| and | fact | flag | hat |
| across | land | hand | stamp |
| man | mass | rat | flat |
| wax | black | fat | attack |
| bad | sad | animal | metal |
| animal | metal | across | canvas |

1

**was** **is**

Ann and the cat

A man sent Ann a black cat.
Ann kept the cat in a bag.
Ann was bad.
A man let the cat get from the bag.
Ann is sad at the loss.

---

B

| 1 | 2 | 3 |
|---|---|---|
| B | B | B |
| but | back | bit |
| rub | bag | band |
| band | best | bed |
| bell | box | brick |
| bulb | black | bent |
| bucket | button | bucket |

**2**

**be** **put** **puts** **'s**

Ben and the pig

A man sent Ben a pig.
Ben put the pig in a box.
Ben's pig is Bill.
Bill will be kept in the box.
Bill's box has a lock.

---

C

| 1 | 2 | 3 |
|---|---|---|
| C | C | C |
| act | back | brick |
| crack | trick | cup |
| cat | clock | neck |
| cup | lock | black |
| sock | stick | ticket |
| and | bucket | attack |
| credit | canvas | second |
| cotton | public | cat |

**3**

**come comes came to**

Come to bed

Bob comes and gets the clock.
Ben had the bricks.
Ann puts the black cat in its bed.
Ben will put the bricks in the box.
Ann and Ben will be put to bed.
Bob came to put us to bed.
Come, Ann and Ben.

---

**D**

| 1 | 2 | 3 |
|---|---|---|
| D | D | D |
| did | send | and |
| end | sand | band |
| dog | drop | red |
| bad | hand | sends |
| send | dust | land |
| wind | bed | dress |
| hard | red | sad |

4

**do ? does**

Did Don come in?

Did Ann let the dog in?
Bob's dog does not come in.
Bob's dog is Don.
Don has a band on his neck.
Did Don come in?
Don did come in, but Bob will put him back in his box.

---

E

| 1 | 2 | 3 | 4 |
|---|---|---|---|
| E | E | E | E |
| went | sends | well | end |
| smell | bell | neck | red |
| step | send | rest | help |
| kept | best | dress | left |
| let | sent | yes | west |
| test | egg | pen | wet |
| lets | get | self | sex |
| bed | leg | stem | bent |

5

**he** **she** **of**

Ben and the steps

Ben got on the steps and he put up a flag.
Come off the steps, Ben.
Ben had a slip from the steps and he got a stiff leg.
Ann will get help.
Ann will come back and she will get him a cup of milk.
Ben, is the leg stiff ?
Ben will be put to bed till the leg is well.

---

F

| 1 | 2 |
|---|---|
| F | F |
| from | off |
| fact | lift |
| flag | flat |
| stiff | left |
| if | self |
| flat | soft |

6

**for** **able**

Ben and the cat

Ann has a cat.
Fluff is Ann's cat and she is a black cat.
Ben has come for Fluff, and he will put Fluff in a bag.
Ann will not let Ben get the cat.
Ben is bad.
Ann has put Fluff in a box.
Ben is not able to get Fluff, and he goes off.

---

G

| 1 | 2 |
| --- | --- |
| G | G |
| grip | grass |
| bag | egg |
| gun | pig |
| dog | flag |
| leg | grip |
| glass | leg |

7

**go goes gone**

Don and the stick

Ann will go to get the dog.
Ben goes to get the dog and he has a stick.
Don is not a bad dog.
He will come if Ben has not got a stick.
Ben has put his stick on the grass, but the dog has gone off.

---

H

H

had
his
help
hand
hat
have
her

8

**have** **her**

Ann and her dress

Ann has on her cotton dress.
Ann will have a silk dress.
But she will not put it on to go for a run.
Her dress will be red, and it will be her best dress.
Ann will have a red hat and a red dress.
Ann will put on her red dress and her red hat.

---

I

| 1 | 2 | 3 | 4 |
|---|---|---|---|
| I | I | I | I |
| did | bit | will | mist |
| in | grip | kick | print |
| till | ink | kiss | pig |
| if | lip | lift | stick |
| still | skin | limit | ill |
| slip | stiff | milk | silk |
| swim | tin | trick | twist |
| wind | brick | pin | ticket |
| solid | prison | list | linen |

9

**I give gave gives**

Ben and his cut lip

Ben had a slip and got a cut on his lip.
Ann will come and give him help.
I will go and get her.
A bad man gave Ben a kick.
Ann gives him a lift.
He has a bad cut on his lip.
Give him a kiss, he is sad.

---

J

*No lists*

10

**see seen saw**

Don and Fluff

I see a rat.
See it go.
Don has seen it and he has gone to get it.
He has got a grip of its back.
The rat got a bit of skin from the dog's neck.
But Don did not let the rat go.
Fluff saw the rat and went off.

Fluff is back, and she sees that a bit of skin is off Don's neck.
Fluff is sad and gives Don's neck a kiss.

---

K

| 1 | 2 | 3 |
|---|---|---|
| K | K | K |
| back | crack | kick |
| kiss | milk | silk |
| trick | stick | brick |
| skin | lock | neck |
| basket | sock | black |
| crack | bucket | ticket |

11

**keep** **keeps**

The pig in the box

Ben keeps a lock on the box.
His pig is in the box.
If the lock is not on the box the pig will be able to go.
He will get from his box and go off.
Ben will have to get a stick to get him back.
It is best to keep the lock on the box.
If the pig is not able to go for a run he will get fat.

## L

| 1 | 2 | 3 | 4 |
|---|---|---|---|
| L | L | L | L |
| let | lets | will | till |
| well | milk | self | smell |
| bulb | flag | lip | help |
| land | lift | list | loss |
| plant | silk | bell | clock |
| leg | lock | black | last |
| ill | flat | left | metal |
| public | vessel | linen | complex |

## 12

**say** **says** **said**

Bob's pot-plant

Bob put a plant in a pot.
" It will come up," he said.
" It will come up if it is kept wet," said Ben.
" I will keep it wet," says Bob.
" I say he will not keep his plant wet," says Ann.
He did not keep his plant wet, and the plant did not come up.

He and Don went for runs, and the plant was not kept wet.
But Ann saw the plant and kept it wet, and in the end it came up.

---

M

| 1 | 2 |
|---|---|
| M | M |
| am | from |
| man | mass |
| milk | mist |
| smell | swim |
| map | pump |
| stamp | stem |
| animal | limit |
| metal | animal |

13

**made** **make** **makes** **with**

A map of Africa

Bob has made a map.
It is a map of Africa.
He made it with a pen.

Ann and Ben see the map.
" I will make a map of Africa with a pen," says Ann.
Ann gets a pen to make her map.
" I will see the map made," says Ben.
Ann makes a map and puts it up for us to see.
" Make a map, Ben, as Ann has done."
But he is not able to get his map done.

---

**N**

| 1<br>N | 2<br>N | 3<br>N | 4<br>N |
|---|---|---|---|
| went | and | plant | tin |
| send | not | print | wind |
| sends | end | run | ant |
| sent | land | sand | band |
| in | man | sun | gun |
| hand | neck | nut | pen |
| pin | skin | animal | bent |
| button | cotton | even | event |
| linen | insect | present | sudden |

14

**take** **took**

A sand man

Ben has made a man of sand.
Bob gave him help.
Ben and Bob took sand, put it in a mass, and made a man from it.
" I see a crack in the sand man," said Ben.
" Go and get a bucket full of sand, Ann."
Ann takes her tin bucket and goes and gets sand for the crack in the sand man.
Ben's sand man has a stick in his hand and a bag on his back.
" Take the stick from the man's hand and give him a flag," says Ann.

---

O

| 1 | 2 | 3 |
|---|---|---|
| O | O | O |
| got | stop | drop |
| soft | from | top |
| lock | across | off |
| box | pot | not |
| dog | rod | loss |
| profit | sock | cotton |
| across | second | solid |

15

**may** **when** **tea**

Ben's clock

Ben has a clock.
" Does the clock go, Ben?" said Bob.
" It goes," said Ben.
" It says when to get up and when to go to bed."
" I get up when the sun comes up from his rest," said Bob.
" I have a clock, and I do not have to see the sun," said Ben.
" I see from the clock when to get up."
" May I see the clock?" said Ann.
" See, Ann, it says: 'Come to tea'," says Ben.
" Let us go to tea."

---

P

| 1 | 2 | 3 |
|---|---|---|
| P | P | P |
| kept | print | cup |
| let | slip | drop |
| grip | step | lip |
| help | stop | pen |
| plant | top | pig |
| pin | pot | pump |
| stamp | prison | public |

16

**me** **good** **my**

Fluff in bed

Ben was in bed and Fluff came to see him.
Fluff is Ann's black cat.
He got on Ben's bed and gave him a rub.
Ben put him in the bed and Fluff gave a 'p-r-r-r.'
" Have you seen my cat?" said Ann.
" I have not seen him," said Ben.
But Ann saw a bit of black Fluff in the bed.
" O, she is in the bed. Let me get her," she said.
" Fluff is not a good cat to get in beds.
Give me my cat and I will take him off," said Ann.
" Come, Fluff, Ben is ill, and he may not have cats in bed."

Q

*No lists*

17

**they** **them** **no**

Ann gets the eggs

Bob and Ben have gone to get in the eggs.

Let us go and give them help.
Quick, Ann, get a basket and let us get eggs as Bob and Ben do.
Let us go to the front, they have gone to the left.
I see Bob is back.
" Did you get the eggs, Ben?"
" No, I saw no eggs, so I was not able to get them," said Ben.
" Did you get the eggs, Ann?" says Bob.
" Yes, I got six eggs," says Ann.
See the eggs in Ann's basket.

---

R

| 1 | 2 |
|---|---|
| R | R |
| from | red |
| print | rest |
| run | drop |
| dress | trick |
| rod | grip |
| brick | rat |
| crack | rub |
| credit | across |
| prison | profit |

18

**are** **we** **by**

Animals in a net

An ant went for a run and saw a rat.

The rat was in a net, and was not able to get from it.

" O," said Rat. " Ant, give me help."

" It is sad, but I am not able to give help," said Ant.

" I was put in the net by a bad dog," said Rat.

" Give the end a pull and I may be able to get from the net."

" I will do my best," said Ant.

He gave a pull,* but he had a slip.

" O, I am in the net," he said.

" It is sad, we are in the net for the bad dog to get," said Rat.

---

[1] The sound of the 'u' is the same as in " put."

S

| 1 | 2 | 3 |
|---|---|---|
| S | S | S |
| loss | yes | lets |
| mass | has | puts |
| mist | kiss | dust |
| self | sand | rest |
| stick | slip | silk |
| soft | dress | twist |
| prison | stem | stamp |
| sudden | sad | stiff |
| us | across | second |

19

**you** **your** **out**

Ann and the pig

" Ann, Ann, come quick, and get a grip of a stick.
I will take the top off my pig-box.
If he comes out give him a kick," said Ben.
" No, no, I will not give your pig a kick.
I will not have a stick," said Ann.
Ben gave a stamp.
" Ann, you are bad. Will you not give me help?"

" No, not if I have to give your pig a kick," said Ann.
" Let him get out and go for a run. He will come back.
You are not good to your pig, Ben.
He is not able to get out for a run."
" He may not come back if I let him out," said Ben.

" Yes, he will, you will see," said Ann.

---

T

| 1 | 2 | 3 | 4 | 5 | 6 |
|---|---|---|---|---|---|
| T | T | T | T | T | T |
| went | kept | let | lets | put | puts |
| sent | act | till | but | still | not |
| west | at | bit | dust | fact | lift |
| tax | plant | print | rest | step | stop |
| ant | test | tin | top | trick | twist |
| rat | cat | hat | net | nut | top |
| flat | stamp | stem | stick | cut | fat |
| ten | stiff | wet | bent | left | soft |
| metal | attack | button | cotton | credit | limit |
| dust | present | profit | regret | ticket | bucket |

20

**what** **why**

The bad dog

The man went out for a run with his dog.
He saw Bob and Ann.
They were out to get nuts, and Don was with them.
Don saw the man's animal and made a run at it.
Bob got him off with a stick.
Ann let her basket of nuts go from her hand and went to the man for help.
" But why did you not let your dog go for a run with my dog?" said the man.
" This is a bad animal and he will make an attack on your dog if we let him," said Bob.
" See what I have done with my nuts," said Ann.
" O, that is sad, we will put them back in the basket for you," said the man.
" You are good," said Ann.

U

| 1 | 2 |
|---|---|
| U | U |
| cut | but |
| jump | dust |
| sudden | rub |
| pump | sun |
| public | bulb |
| bucket | cut |
| disgust | gun |
| nut | us |

21

**here** **there** **where**

Fluff takes a jump

Ben and Ann were at tea.
Ben had a cup of tea in his hand.
The cat took a quick jump and sent the cup from Ben's hand.
" O, the bad cat.
She has gone off. Where did she go?
Do you see her, Ann?"
" No, I do not see her."
" There she is.
Come here, Fluff."

"Fluff is sad that she was bad.
Give her a kiss, she will be good.
Put her in her box and she will say 'p-r-r-r.'
Let us get back to tea at last."

---

V

*No lists*

22

**any** **some**

Ann makes tea

Nan is out and Ann will make tea.
She has put a vessel on the gas.
"O," says Ann.
"What is it, Ann?"
"There is a smell of gas."
"Quick, put some wax in the crack."
"Good, the crack is gone. That is well," said Ann.
"Here is the tea pot."
"I will make the tea and we will have eggs for tea," said Ann.

" Good," say Ben and Bob.
" Have some tea yourself, Ann."
" Give me your cup, Ben, you have not got any tea," says Ann.
" It is good to have tea when Nan is not here," said Ben.
" We do not have to be good."
" O, yes, you do," says Ann.

---

W

went
wet
twist
will
well
wax
west
swim
wind

23

**only** **over**

We go for a swim

' Get up, get up, Ben," says Bob.
" The sun is up and we are to go for a swim. Where is your clock, Ben ?
You said it said when to get up."
" O, it has come to a stop," said Ben.
" Ann, he said his clock said when to get up, and it has come to a stop," said Bob.
" He will not be able to come with us, will he Bob?" said Ann.
" Do not go without me, I will get up and come. Here I am," said Ben.
" I will only take a swim to the flat bit of land," said Ann.
" We will go over and back," said Ben.
" I will be here when you get back," says Ann.

---

X

*No lists*

24

**who** **so**

The tax man

The man has come for the tax.
She does not give it to him, she has not any to give.
She will be sent to prison.
The man gives her no help, and she has nowhere to go.
It is so sad for her.
If we give the man the tax he will let her go.
" Here, man, here is your tax, you may let her go."
We will take her back.
She is so sad, she does not see that the man has gone.
Who is she ? Where will she go ?

---

Y

*No lists*

25

**last** **very**

Ann gets wet

" What have you done, Ann?"
" I am very wet," says Ann.
" Come in and get the wet off.
Do not put a dress on till you have got off the last drop of wet.
Give yourself a good rub."
" It is very wet out and I have no umbrella," says Ann.
" When you go I will give you an umbrella, and you will not get wet."
" You are very good to me," said Ann.
Ann is not able to go till the last drop of wet is off.
" You were very good, but I will go back," says Ann.

---

Z

*No lists*

26

**little move old**

Bob does a good act

See the little old man.
He has a stick and his back is bent.
O, he has let go his stick.
" Do not make a move, old man.
I will get your stick.
Here it is.
Put it in your hand and get a good grip of it.
I will give you help till you get across, then you will not have a slip."
" You are good," said the little old man.
" No, I am not good," said Bob.
" But I give help when I am able."
Bob's dog goes across with them.